Building Communities
of Difference

Building Communities
of Difference

HIGHER EDUCATION IN THE
TWENTY-FIRST CENTURY

William G. Tierney

CRITICAL STUDIES IN EDUCATION AND CULTURE SERIES
Edited by Henry A. Giroux and Paulo Freire

BERGIN & GARVEY
Westport, Connecticut • London

This document was prepared partially with financial support from the U.S. Department of Education's Office of Educational Research and Improvement (OERI), Grant R117G0037. The opinions expressed herein do not reflect the position and policy of OERI, and no official endorsement should be inferred.

Library of Congress Cataloging-in-Publication Data

Tierney, William G.
    Building communities of difference : higher education in the twenty-first
century / William G. Tierney.
        p.   cm.—(Critical studies in education and culture series, ISSN 1064–8615)
    Includes bibliographical references and index.
    ISBN 0–89789–312–3.—ISBN 0–89789–313–1 (pbk.)
    1. Education, Higher—United States—Philosophy.   2. Critical
theory.   3. Critical pedagogy—United States.   I. Title.
    II. Series.
    LA227.4.T54   1993
    378'.001—dc20   92–31297

British Library Cataloguing in Publication Data is available.

Library of Congress Catalog Card Number: 92–31297
ISBN: 0–89789–312–3
        0–89789–313–1 (pbk.)
ISSN: 1064–8615

First published in 1993

Bergin & Garvey, 88 Post Road West, Westport, CT 06881
An imprint of Greenwood Publishing Group, Inc.

Printed in the United States of America

The paper used in this book complies with the Permanent Paper
Standard issued by the National Information Standards
Organization (Z39.48–1984).

10 9 8 7 6 5 4 3 2 1

For my friends and colleagues at Penn State University who, despite all odds, are struggling to build a community of difference.

Contents

Foreword

As one of the most important theorists on higher education, Bill Tierney has been engaging the relationship among difference, identity, power, and knowledge for a number of years. What is so commendable about his work is not only the theoretical energy, determination, and courage he has displayed in confronting the New Right assault on higher education, but also his ongoing attempts to develop alternative theories and strategies that are at once accessible and inspiring for administrators, teachers, and students involved in academia.

Building Communities of Difference represents a remarkable achievement for a number of reasons. First, it exemplifies the range and depth of Tierney's intellectual energy. As a restless, border intellectual, Tierney constantly crosses diverse disciplinary boundaries and fashions new connections and insights out of a variety of theoretical discourses. Second, he constructs the terms of his language outside of the smug and vitriolic sectarianism that has come to characterize all too many theorists of difference in higher education. Rather than denounce others who share similar theoretical positions, Tierney looks for the articulations and relevancies among different strands of radical work and attempts to engage and translate disparate discourses into terms that productively shape public debate and policy. Determined to expand conversations and public debate, Tierney refuses to use a language forged in anger and sectarianism. The result, in part, is a model of what it means to be a public intellectual working in higher education today. Third, Tierney is always aware of the interconnection between difference, power, and ethics. By analyzing how differences are constituted in and mediated across sexual orientation, ethnicity, race, class, and gender, he makes visible through a series of textual studies and case studies how such differences are constituted and shaped within the ever contested terrains of power that construct institutions of higher education. Difference does not collapse simply into an expanding range of significations in this book, it is always treated historically and relationally as a struggle over power, signs, and identities. Finally, Tierney moves brilliantly between theory and practice so as to make clear how theory is lived out in specific, concrete struggles that mark the institutional and ideological terrains of power in higher education. For Tierney, theory is a practice that is constantly informing one's beliefs, actions, and practices; at the same time it is more than a matter of epistemology and aesthetics, it is also a borderland where conversations begin, differences confront each other, hopes are initiated, and social struggles are waged.

What is so extraordinary about Tierney's work is the way in which he has combined the real, symbolic, and imagined boundaries of critical theory and postmodern discourses into a viable cultural politics. Fusing critical theory's concern with politics and ethics with a postmodern understanding of difference, Tierney rewrites the possibilities for political and pedagogical struggle as part of a broader effort to democratize and pluralize higher education and other public spheres. Politics, community, and identity are at the heart of Tierney's transformative project. But as he is quick to point out, modernism's project of scientific rationality must be rewritten, just as postmodern's concern with creating a new language cannot be accepted as an end in itself. Instead he calls for a "mutual dialogue of respect" that combines modernism's notion of agency with postmodernism's recognition of the fluidity and multiplicity of identity. He wants educators and cultural workers to understand how identities work, how their multiplicities can be negotiated and hybridized to affirm the power of difference, and how a unity in difference can be developed through a notion of meaningful community rooted in the public discourse and lived experience of democracy, citizenship, and human rights.

There is another important element in Tierney's work that sets him apart from a number of other educational theorists. He recognizes that hope is the precondition for individual and collective agency. But this is not a hope that erases history, power, and politics. On the contrary, Tierney is not content to build merely a theoretical argument for hope as a precondition for critical agency and change. With great enunciative energy, he is also brilliantly attentive to how hope works through the narratives and voices of Native Americans, friends who have AIDS, gay and lesbian students, colleagues, and faculty and students whom he engages in dialogue and analysis. In my view, for Tierney, hope becomes the redeemed discourse, a fleeting image of freedom and possibility, one that is often dismissed by many educators as that which is unverifiable and, thus, unknowable. Hope, in this sense, is both the language of uncertainty and the precondition for action; it offers neither prescriptions nor recipes. Instead, it points to the value of a discourse whose value lies in what it suggests about the stirring of imagination, the possibilities that are often felt and deeply experienced in the need to struggle against all odds. It is part of the moral fabric that gives educators, students, and others a reason to raise the question "What for?" It points to the necessity for political and pedagogical projects that locate teachers, students, and other cultural workers as subjects rather than objects of history. It posits a refusal to perceive human life as meaningless, education as futile, and struggle as another fashion hype. But at the same time Tierney's notion of hope offers no answers. It occupies the terrain of uncertainty while affirming issues of purpose and meaning as central to what it means to know, act, live, and construct communities of difference and love with others.

In attempting to rescue a viable notion of political agency from modernism, and a respectful notion of difference from postmodernity, Tierney attempts to write the concept of the ethical back into pedagogical and public discourse. Refusing a narrow and often essentialized notion of caring, he connects the issue of solidarity to the concept of "agape," a notion of selfless love that rejects both an apocalyptic emptiness and a cynical refusal to engage in social dialogue around the needs and welfare of others. How we conceive of identity in this perspective is fundamentally about how communities are named, what is excluded, and what the political consequences are for such actions. Identity and community are about more than the quest for visibility, they are also about recognizing that who we are is inextricably bound up with the identities of others. Moreover, while such identities are always constituted in differences, they run the risk of an anti-democratic separatism unless they share a moral content that demands an ongoing conversation, dialogue, and trust that cuts across and transcends various particularisms.

Throughout this book Tierney draws upon a wealth of ethnographic material to engage what he calls his long range goal: "How might we as educators develop communities of difference where agape and hope are central characteristics?" Whether he is looking at the concretely lived dynamics of community at Deep Springs College, or assessing the relationship between organizational structures and critical leadership at Sherman College, Tierney is always attuned to dissecting the dynamics of empowerment and trying to analyze the conditions that might enable administrators, teachers, and students in higher education to be able to imagine otherwise in order to act with courage and passion. Moreover, he is critically attentive to the content and contexts of his own interaction with others, and to analyzing the implications of the politics of his own location. But recognizing one's own partiality does not dispel Tierney's firm conviction about being politically committed. In fact, for Tierney, it is precisely an understanding of one's sense of location and commitment that provides the basis for taking a position while simultaneously being open to dialogue, understanding, and the voices of others.

Beneath these concerns is Tierney's fierce belief in the necessity to forge a new understanding between difference and community, but there is more at work in *Building Communities of Difference* than the virtue of theoretical illumination. While drawing on an impressive array of case studies, Tierney also offers a number of concrete insights into how communities of difference can be developed in higher education. This is a book that breaks new ground in a double sense. First, it makes accessible the best insights of critical theory and postmodern discourse. Second, it intertwines the necessity of theory with the reality of the concrete in ways that provide a language of critique, practice, and possibility. I know of no other book on higher education that contains such wisdom, intelligence, and compassion.

                                                            Henry A. Giroux

Building Communities
of Difference

Chapter One

Toward the Postmodern: Communities of Difference

Haltingly and with a good deal of trepidation, those of us involved in American higher education approach the twenty-first century beset with a variety of daunting problems. Except at a handful of the most well-endowed institutions, colleges and universities face decaying physical plants and increased demands for scientific and technological laboratories that will meet the needs of a rapidly changing environment. The revenue to maintain buildings, much less build new ones, is nonexistent. Students and their families are less willing and less able to pay for the costs of higher education. Reductions in financial aid from the public sector have affected students' prospects for receiving grants or loans. Public institutions must also deal with dramatically reduced revenues from the states and the federal government.

Vitriolic attacks on the professoriate seem to take place on an almost daily basis. The faculty, it is claimed, are out of step with the needs of American society. Their research is irrelevant, they are paid too much, and they are disengaged from the lives of their students and the community. Petty departmental politics or internecine warfare among different colleges stymies any hope for constructive change; moreover, according to some critics, the faculty are trying to foist their left-wing ideology on students through a curriculum that has lost coherence and rigor.

Faculty, on the other hand, assert that many students are ill-prepared for postsecondary coursework and that the institutions are incapable of dealing with diverse student populations. Faculty also claim that the system of promotion and tenure places unfair demands on individuals and rewards meaningless activities and that far too much time is spent on trivial committee work. Faculty salaries have not kept pace with inflation, and poorly paid part-time faculty positions continue to grow at the expense of full-time colleagues. The view that the administration in general, and the president in particular, are capable of leadership is met with serious skepticism.

Among other concerns, no one is pleased with huge classes in which hundreds of students passively sit and take notes from a lecturer who may be a teaching assistant. Students and parents demand more active learning. Faculty decry their inability to engage students on an interpersonal basis. Administrators struggle to find the funds to replace retiring faculty. State legislators require colleges and universities to develop assessment measures to gauge how well an institution is teaching its students.

Simply stated, public confidence in American higher education is at an all-time low, and solutions to the problems seem elusive, if not impossible. Indeed, the tenor of debate about American higher education is riddled with cynicism and despair. A sense of commitment or of common purpose is absent. The belief that postsecondary education is a public good that aids in the development of the individual, the community, and society itself seems to have been lost in an age when resources are finite.

In this text, I argue that the central problems that face academe are neither fiscal nor structural; rather, the central challenge that currently confronts us is a moral one. I do not question these very serious conditions, and I intend to offer several specific proposals about how we might solve them. My ideas, however, derive from a specific philosophical stance that I must first elaborate so that my subsequent comments make sense. For example, suggestions that we need to focus on student-oriented outcomes to ensure academic quality or that we should increase part-time faculty to save costs are not merely practical, "real-world" solutions; they are also emblematic of institutional strategies and beliefs about our organizations.

Accordingly, in the last chapter of the book, I develop a series of proposals about what actions we might take to solve some of the problems that currently confront academe. These proposals logically derive from the analyses and information offered in earlier chapters. Over the past two years, I have been involved in a series of case studies of postsecondary institutions; these case studies account for Chapters 4, 5, and 6. Each analysis deals with the structure of decision making in colleges and universities. I highlight both those whose voices are included and those whose are excluded as institutions struggle to make decisions about the directions they intend to take. These chapters underscore how academic structures give prominence to some ideas and constituencies, and silence others.

In Chapters 1, 2, and 3, I undertake three tasks. To begin, I will outline the theoretical scaffolding of my thought. In particular, I will focus on what I mean by *postmodernism* and *critical theory*. I need to state at the outset that I enter into a contested dialogue here, for I try to unite these elements, whereas some might say that the theoretical movements are in opposition to one another. I argue the opposite. In doing so, I spend a good deal of time discussing the concepts of difference, identity, and community. I consider how the notions of postmodernism and critical theory influence how we conceive of educational institutions, and I offer a definition of community based on the concept of *difference*, rather than similarity.

In Chapter 2, I offer a case study of a small liberal arts institution—Deep Springs College. My purpose in doing so is to provide an educational mirror to guide the ensuing discussion of what I mean by a "community of difference." I extend the concepts of postmodernism and critical theory by defining *educational empowerment*, and I consider the cultural determinants of the organization that have enabled it to remain radical rather than regress to the norm. The third chapter concentrates on the concepts of identity and difference by way of a series of interviews with gay and lesbian faculty at one university. I speak about the ideology of silencing and the culture of the norm to highlight how we might reconceive of individuals in academic institutions.

My goal for the text is twofold. By way of ethnographic case studies, I hope first to highlight some of the struggles that confront different institutions; the theoretical framework offers a different way of interpreting the problems that beset these colleges and universities and enables us to consider how organizational change might take place. I also intend to develop solutions that redirect our resources and energies away from individualism and competitive models and toward what I shall call "organizational agape."

POSTMODERNISM AND CRITICAL THEORY

To some, an idea born at the height of modernism—critical theory—has little in common with modernism's successor—postmodernism. How can a framework that works from modernist suppositions be wedded to a theory that rejects those assumptions? And more importantly for my purpose here, how do postmodernism and critical theory help us deal with the problems that exist in higher education? I will answer those questions by describing five axes of contention that underscore the differences between postmodernism and critical theory and by discussing how I utilize them for conceptualizing practice in postsecondary institutions.

I also need to point out how I make use of critical theory and postmodernism in this chapter and text. Briefly, as employed here, critical theory is an attempt to understand the oppressive aspects of society in order to generate societal and individual transformation (Fay, 1987). Postmodernism challenges the cultural politics of modernist notions of rationality, norms, and identity. Obviously, both theories are contested terrain where different authors subscribe to differing interpretations of what they mean by these terms. As I elaborate, I am not particularly interested in entering into such a debate; my purpose here is to offer my own interpretation of both theories as an analytical framework for action in postsecondary institutions. If our actions derive from our ideas and beliefs, then it is incumbent on me as an author to enable the reader to see how I arrive at the conclusions I develop in the last chapter. To be sure, the data that accounts for the case studies influenced how I think about educational institutions, but as with any investigation, the theoretical models that I carry in my head also influence how I see the world. Accordingly, I consider these postmodern and critical axes of contention as conversational points to highlight the framework I utilize in the text.

By *axes of contention*, I mean those principles that each theory holds that seem to be in conflict with one another, so that if one believes one proposition of critical theory, then one ought not be able to hold the counter proposition of postmodernism. To demonstrate these axes, I draw upon examples from everyday life rather than the abstract theorizing we have come to associate with both approaches. Indeed, one curiosity of both theories is that they often seem immune to public discourse and to the development of a language that is accessible to individuals other than academics; at the same time, one of the key components of both ideas concerns engagement with that public.

Critical theory, for example, has its roots in the 1920s when the "Frankfurt School" in Germany sought to develop a project of human emancipation. As Seyla Benhabib notes, critical theory shares "the intentions of the traditional teachings of ethics and politics to unite the claim of reason with the happiness and freedom of individuals and the justice of the collectivity" (1986, p. 2). That is, critical theorists want to determine the oppressive features of society; once they are understood, the intent is to develop the conditions under which those who are oppressed might be able to liberate themselves.

The attempt to understand society in this manner means that critical theorists reject the positivist notion of knowledge and science. As William Foster explains, "Logical positivism asserted that only scientific knowledge, which was verifiable in principle, was true knowledge and could be expressed in logical and therefore true form. . . . Values, ethics and morality [were] simply matters of assertion or preference" (1986, p. 35). Instead, critical theory asserts that all knowledge is socially and historically determined and a consequence of power.

Given the assumptions about knowledge and the purpose of research, the concept of power becomes infused with a concern for empowerment. I discuss educational empowerment at greater length in Chapter 2, but for now what is important to note is critical theory's central focus on conducting research and building structures that enhance empowerment and democracy. As Henry Giroux comments:

Critical theory does not equate the struggle for public life with the narrowly defined interests of the group, irrespective of the nature of their power or the legitimacy of their interest. [Critical theory] links schooling to the imperatives of democracy, views teachers as transformative intellectuals, and makes the notion of democratic difference central (1988b, p. 164).

Postmodernism, on the other hand, rejects the assumption that through reason we will be able to achieve agreement about the nature of truth or oppression. "Postmodernism," Andrew Gitlin notes, "is completely indifferent to the questions of consistency and continuity. . . . It neither embraces nor criticizes, but beholds the world blankly, with a knowingness that dissolves feeling and commitment into irony" (1989, p. 52). Thus, rather than struggle to enable groups to overthrow anything, postmodernism attempts to develop multivocality and to understand difference.

The forms that postmodernists want to employ to develop this difference often exist outside of the academic mainstream. As Patti Lather comments, postmodernists "interrupt academic norms by writing inside of another logic, a logic that displaces expectations of linearity, clear authorial voice and closure" (1989, p. 8). In doing so, postmodernists often eschew the search for clarity or persuasion through rational logic because absolutes no longer exist. Any theoretical framework that makes claims as a metanarrative needs to be interrogated and exposed.

Not only are metanarratives rejected, but the idea of difference becomes a central organizing concept. "Because all signifiers are mere constructions," point out Burbules and Rice, "there is no clear reason to grant any one special significance or value over others" (1991, p. 396). The point here is that individual and group differences are not merely way stations on the road to consensus; rather, since agreement to principles will not be reached—and ought not to be a goal—one highlights how people talk past one another and how multiple representations exist within society.

We have become a society where social identity is formed through the mass media. The multiplicity of images that cascade in upon us defeat any suggestion that a reality exists or can ever be known; instead, a hyperreality has taken hold, where multiple significations occur simultaneously. "We can no longer relate our understanding of the self to the images we see," conclude William Tierney and Robert Rhoads, "but instead we have become images ourselves created by complex social and cultural forces" (forthcoming).

Thus, one might assume that critical theory's concern with changing the oppressive aspects of life and postmodernism's emphasis on moving outside academic norms would unite both concepts in a desire to reach the public. Yet the opposite has been the case. Indeed, I might add that the conservative right's ability to capture the discourse about education and society in the last decade has come about in part because of a successful manipulation of the dialogue and media images that postmodernity critiques; at the same time, critical theorists and postmodernists have been equally abysmal in moving our ideas into a public arena.

What follows are five points that highlight tensions between critical theory and postmodernity, delineate differences with the conservative critique, and in doing so, place me in a particular discourse. My hope is that once I have pointed out how these axes function, we will be better able to develop practical and policy-oriented positions that will stand in contrast to the conservative critique of academe. In part, the left's response to the conservative agenda has been to argue about the inadequacy of its theoretical ideas. Although such a response is warranted, we also are obliged to move one step further and necessarily translate these theoretical notions into public debate. Accordingly, I will first lay out the theoretical framework, then analyze different case studies using this lens, and subsequently suggest alternative policies.

AXES OF CONTENTION

Boundaries/Border Zones

"Some of the ways in which I identify myself," writes Audre Lorde, "make it difficult for you to hear me" (1985, p. 3). Lorde writes to her black sisters about the difficulty she finds in being heard because she is lesbian. She continues by arguing that "unity does not require that we be identical to each other" (1985, p. 3). The importance Lorde places on difference parallels postmodernism's emphasis on difference, and critical theory's desire for concerted action; however, postmodernists often conceptualize difference as if it is constituted by impermeable boundaries that cannot be crossed and will not be understood. Critical theory, based on modernist ideas of reason, in general has not dealt with difference. It seems helpful, then, to combine both theoretical schemas to concentrate on how difference can be utilized to develop a framework for change.

As I use the idea of difference here, I reject the notion that differences across groups create an inability to understand one another. Rather than boundaries that cannot be crossed, I develop the idea of "border zones." "A borderland," writes Gloria Anzaldua, "is a vague and undetermined place created by the emotional residue of an unnatural boundary. It is in a constant state of transition" (1987, p. 3). Border zones are cultural areas infused with differences. By "cultural areas," I do not simply mean geographic locations, as if one locale is a cultural area and another is not. *Culture* pertains to the set of symbolic processes, ideologies, and sociohistorical contexts that are situated in an arena of struggle and multiple interpretations.

Part of the postmodern critique has been to point out how we have too often conceived of differences as categories that differ from the norm. In this light, difference simply pertains to those who are different from the norm—black people are different from white people; gay people are different from heterosexuals; women are different from men. As postmodernists have pointed out, the problem with this configuration is that it places those of us who are different constantly in relation to what is conceived as "normal" and something to be desired.

Indeed, one of the problems of modernist versions of critical theory is the assumption that simply through dialogue we will be able to understand one another's differences. As Giroux notes, "Understanding the limits of a particular position, engaging its contradictory messages, or extending its insights beyond the limits of particular experiences is lost in this position" (1988b, p. 164). We lose the relational aspect in which individuals are engaged, so we are incapable of interrogating difference from the perspective of power, knowledge, and authority. Instead, we interrogate difference merely as if we are developing a taxonomy of difference.

Postmodernists, however, have highlighted the multiple images in society that send out messages reinforcing powerful norms, which, in turn, situate difference in terms of power and knowledge. "By insisting on the multiplicity of social positions," notes Giroux, "[postmodernism] has seriously challenged the political closure of modernity with its divisions between the center and the margins and in doing so has made room for those groups generally defined as the excluded others" (1988b, p. 166). Postmodernism, then, is helpful for decoding any number of contemporary images.

The infamous Willie Horton ad during the 1988 presidential campaign, for example, offered a picture of a black man that painted for society what would happen to "our way of life" if we voted for one candidate as opposed to another. Conservative images of leather-jacketed gay men walking hand in hand provide a consistent picture of how different "they" are from the rest of "us." Some of the images etched in the nation's consciousness during the Los Angeles riots of 1992 revealed irrational mobs looting and burning their own neighborhoods.

The problem with images such as these is more than simply that they are distortions of humanity—as if nicer imagery would solve the trouble that such portraits cause. The fundamental issue is mainstream society's inability to disassociate norms from differences. In this light, we see someone as a "lesbian" or a "Native American," but we do not categorize their counterparts as a "heterosexual woman" or Caucasian. The concern, of course, is that when we watch a film that has a lesbian murderer, we generalize that that is the way all lesbians behave; yet when we watch a film where a white man is a murderer, we are able to disassociate the individual's characteristics from the act in which he is involved. We see domestic violence occur in a working-class family and believe that is the way the working class lives; when we see violence in a middle-class family, we disassociate that violence from the middle class because that is not our image of the middle class.

These images are often indirect rather than confrontational. We see gay men in film or on TV when the issue pertains to a gay theme; we often think of AIDS as a central gay theme, but we do not see gay men in the full array of their lives as individuals who work and inhabit everyday existence. Hispanic people appear in stories about what it means to be Hispanic, but they seem incapable of transcending their own cultural configurations. Those people in the norm, however, appear as they are—in any number of situations, from crises to mundane activities, from life's defining moments such as birth and death, to life's humdrum daily acts such as taking children to school. The observer of these scenes of daily life learns that those who inhabit the norm are able to exist in a cultural vacuum, whereas those individuals who "have culture" seem unable to shed it.

Postmodernism is helpful not only to deconstruct images, but also to question the multiple meanings we give to words. We see, for example, particular definitions of ideological values such as "courage," "honor," and the like. These values are associated with norms, and by inference, those individuals who inhabit the center. Again, there will be images of those who are different acting courageously or honorably; however, the image that is projected is that a specific "Indian" is acting honorably as opposed to all native people acting in such a way. When we see the white woman act in similar fashion, we are able to assume she is acting in a manner that is typical of such people.

And since those people who inhabit the center do not "have culture," we implicitly teach that to act and speak, indeed to think and love, in a particular way that is associated with one's culture is aberrant. The norms of speech teach us that one dialect is better than another, and that a deep voice is preferable to a higher inflection. If love between men and women is normal, then any other kind of relationship becomes abnormal. Thus, the culture of the Native American that teaches a child to speak in a native tongue will disadvantage the child. Women learn to speak like men so that they will be able to gain the influence and prestige associated with male positions in society. And psychotherapy is thought of as a way to help the homosexual overcome the "disability" of same-sex desire. The aspiration for each of these attributes, for example, is seen not as a matter of gaining other cultural qualities, but of shedding one's own culture. To be sure, we encourage people to keep certain cultural qualities, but only insofar as they do not create significant differences from the norm.

Although postmodernists wish to uncover and expose the pervasive power of the norm, that should not imply that the postmodern critique desires to do away with the diversity that exists in society. And yet, postmodernism bereft of a critical theory does not give us a sense of what we are to do with these multiple meanings and images. Obviously, I am not suggesting that we should try to develop imagery through which everyone is alike, so that differences such as race, class, gender, and sexual orientation dissolve. The problem with that goal is twofold. On the one hand, the idea that America is a "melting pot" has long since been shown for what it is; those of us who are different are supposed to "melt" into what is normal. *Assimilation, acculturation*, and other code words really imply that those who "have culture" need to lose it. Gay people should be "straight." People of color should adopt "white" definitions of family, community, desire, and so on. Women should assume masculine identities.

On the other hand, to assume that we ought to try to dissolve differences also overlooks the strength that diversity brings to society. Understanding difference affords individuals the possibility not only of understanding other people's lives, but also of coming to terms with how they are situated within society, how their specific identities are framed and shaped by society. This idea of understanding difference is essentially a critical formulation, and it is where some postmodernists and critical theorists might differ; it also underscores how I use critical theory and postmodernism in this text. Just as critical theory has not thoroughly investigated the idea of difference and identity, postmodernism's implicit nihilism and assumption that differences are impossible to bridge seem equally facile.

There are those in the postmodern camp who refuse to consider that dialogue and understanding across differences are possible. Elizabeth Ellsworth, for example, created a heated debate in the *Harvard Educational Review* when she wrote as a postmodernist and attacked critical theorists' attempts at empowerment. "In a racist society and its institutions," she writes, "such debate has not and cannot be 'public' or 'democratic' in the sense of including the views of all affected parties and affording them equal weight and legitimacy" (1989, p. 302). Norms are so powerful, argues Ellsworth, that any attempt at dialogue only fools individuals into thinking that change is possible. Obviously, if such dialogues are impossible, then it is fruitless—if not deceptive—to think of difference as a strength. From this perspective, difference is not a weakness, but it cannot be a strength either; rather, the development of differences takes place merely to create a societal multivocality. That I am incapable of conceiving what such a society might look like is not cause for rejecting the idea, and yet I lose any sense of societal, communal, or individual purpose, meaning, or commitment.

Critical theory's advocacy for empowerment and the development of voice for oppressed people needs to be fused with the postmodern notion of difference. The "development of voice" is not an act or offering that one individual is able to give to another; far too often we have assumed the condescending attitude that "oppressed" people need to be enlightened. Such an assumption only recreates the structures that we are trying to change where the powerful are capable of determining the parameters of reality for the powerless. Instead, I am suggesting that individuals develop their own voices by coming to terms with how the sociocultural forces that surround them have altered, silenced, or distorted their histories. Difference becomes central, norms are decentered, and dialogue remains a possibility. The consequence is that we dissolve boundaries and incorporate the idea of borderlands that we all inhabit. Our struggle is constantly to cross these borders and exist in tolerable discomfort with one another as we confront difference. The reason I mention discomfort is that by its very nature "difference" is discomforting; to engage in dialogue and action with individuals who may have conflicting ideas and constructions about the world is hard work, but as I argue throughout this text, such work creates the conditions for change and what I call *cultural democracy*. Cultural democracy involves the enactment of dialogue and action that are based on a framework of trying to understand and to honor cultural difference, rather than of subjugating such difference to mere attributes of an individual's identity. Renato Rosaldo elaborates:

Our everyday lives are crisscrossed by border zones, pockets, and eruptions of all kinds. Social borders frequently become salient around such lines as sexual orientation, gender, class, race, ethnicity, nationality, age, politics, dress, food, or taste. Along with "our" supposedly transparent cultural selves, such borderlands should be regarded not as analytically empty transitional zones but as sites of creative cultural production (1989, p. 208).

We have, then, one coordinate on which this text is based. I develop educational proposals in which norms are decentered and difference becomes an organizing concept. I assume the critical demand for struggle and the postmodern belief in the power of the norm. I disagree with some postmodernists' assertion that spanning border zones is impossible, and I extend critical theory's notion about understanding differences. The second axis pertains to the possibilities and constraints for action and dialogue.

Individual Constraints/Pluralist Possibility

How we conceive of the individual relates directly to the proposition that we must decenter norms, for if we no longer subscribe to set defini- tions of what counts as "normal," then the idea of individual identity is brought into question. That is, in a postmodern world the way we have come to understand the self has shifted, and, accordingly, how we conceive of groups also must change.

We once held a heroic ideal that assumed certain individuals were capable of single-handedly creating change. Such an idea was born of *romanticism* in which leadership was defined in terms of "great men" who had divine capabilities, and life was ruled by mysterious religious or naturalistic forces. We conceived of power in individualistic terms and believed that the human will was free-floating and capable of producing whatever changes it desired. Individual identity was also fixed, coherent, and determined. Institutions such as the church and state established categories within which individuals fit.

The French philosopher Michel Foucault (1980b) argues that categories such as homosexual/heterosexual were not invented until the late nineteenth century. Even if one argues with Foucault's assertion, we know that a unified sexual identity was assumed from the absence of any discussion prior to the twentieth century. That is, "homosexuality" was an absent category. Similarly, women's history was also absent from intellectual analysis. Thus, in general, the manner in which identity was defined was through a singular, cohesive ideal self.

Modernism and its quest for scientific answers rejected belief in religious or naturalistic truths. Instead, the scientific study of human progress sought to understand by rational analysis "man's" motivations and inner drives. The birth of psychiatry and scientific management are examples of modernism's drive for measurement rather than belief. Nevertheless, modernism still upheld the notion of a singular, cohesive identity. Foucault (1980a) also has been helpful in delineating how modernism's use of power shifted from roles and authority—kings and popes—to that of "disciplinary regimes"—medicine, psychiatry, and economics.

These disciplines utilized norms so that we understood that dichotomies existed—male/female, heterosexual/homosexual, civilized/uncivilized. Modernists tried to understand those who were different in terms of how they differed from the norm. Identity was once again seen as cohesive, and science either tried to understand how to "fix" those who did not fit the modernist version of identity or created labels and analyses to explain the identity flaws. Thus, in one case modernists worked to educate savages with the belief that they could become civilized, and in another case they tried to understand the female psyche.

Ironically, romanticism and modernism offered competing definitions of the individual and identity—one based on religion and myth, the other on reason and science—yet what undergirded both approaches was the belief in human perfectibility and progress. Romanticism tried to save people's souls, and modernism their minds. The assumption was that humankind could improve, that in one fashion or another, we would be better off in the future than we were in the present. One view assumed that the road to improvement was through belief, and proponents of the other view argued that positivism would enable us to prove right from wrong.

Obviously, strains of both ideas reside in society today. I have overstated the case if I have portrayed these epochs as merely linear successions from one century to another. Religious belief rises and falls in periodic twists and turns. Our faith in modern medicine also is subject to scientific failures and successes and societal expectations. As we approach the twenty-first century, we also have residual effects of romanticism and modernism in how we think about the individual and society. The assumption that we can better ourselves, either through belief or reason, has existed through a unified sense of self and what we believe to be knowledge and reason.

One example that might help clarify what I am trying to establish is the concept of sexual orientation. Throughout the twentieth century in America, we have gone back and forth between romantic and modernist beliefs about fixed and stable identities. There are two categories of human beings—men and women—and there is one sexual orientation—heterosexual. To be sure, we have acknowledged that there are sexual variations—transvestites, homosexuals, and the like—but we have either tried to prove through religious documentation that such aberrations are wrong or we have tried to cure these people using scientific methods—psychiatry, medicine, and the law. The ideology of romanticism, then, reaffirms the singular heterosexual self through a religious belief, and the ideology of modernism does the same through a scientific belief.

Another clarifying example pertains to how we have conceived of the American family. Again, our society has defined family relationships in a way familiar to those of us who have a European heritage—mother, father, sister, brother. We have created societal laws and policies that privilege our conception of this family. A man and woman may get married, colleges and universities have "married student housing," and even when we think of a marriage as "failing," we decide if the child should go with the mother or father. Religion defines an unmarried man and woman living together as "living in sin"; science dictates that to take the child away from his or her "natural" parents is cause for harm. In this instance, then, the romantic ideology defines a singular identity based on European beliefs, and modernist ideology does so from a scientific stance.

A third example pertains to AIDS (acquired immunodeficiency syndrome). There are those in the religious world who believe that the disease is God's retribution for sinners. The scientific response has been that a disease is a medical phenomenon that demands a doctor's profes-sional diagnosis and has nothing to do with heaven, hell, and damnation. Once again we see romantic and modernist ideologies at work.

Each of these examples has common assumptions that surround it. When I write that "identity is fixed" or the "self is coherent," I have in mind romantic and modernist portraits from the previous discussion. We assume that gender is defined. We believe that familial relationships are prescribed. We have a particular stance toward the sick. Obviously, with each example, romantic and modernist conceptions differ on how to treat the individual, but both have worked from universalist conceptions of the self.

In their attempt at essentializing categories, what these beliefs have missed, however, is how society has constructed the very categories themselves. Walter Williams' (1992) pathfinding work on sexual diversity in Native American Indian culture has shown us how numerous tribes existed not only with the traditional gender categories of man and woman, but also with a third category of individuals known as the *berdache*. The berdache were respected, spiritual members of society who were physically male and they dressed as women. Williams makes a compelling argument that these individuals ought not to be thought of as men who were homosexual, but instead they need to be considered the way the culture in which they existed defined them—as neither men nor women, but as *berdache*.

Similarly, we know from native societies that familial relationships exist in dramatically different forms than the traditional European version. Native beliefs in the family surely exist, but not as the white world has defined them. Again, romantic and modern notions have offered a fixed construction so that we are able to determine right from wrong. As with the AIDS example, we see how the individual is defined in a specific manner—as a "sinner" or as a diseased person.

A modernist or religious critic rightfully will point out concerns with my portraits. Certainly all religions do not think of people with AIDS as evil, so to characterize all people who have a faith in God in this manner is unfair and deterministic. Scientific organizations declassified homosexuality as an illness over twenty years ago, so to portray science in its turn-of-the-century format is equally pernicious. If anything, one might argue, a history of science only reaffirms our belief in scientific progress, for as we have learned more, our ideas have changed. Some of those who subscribe to romantic notions might point out that their beliefs are also compassionate, and those who are modernist would rightfully ask why I would bring into question the medical treatment of disease. As Diane Ravitch asks, if someone broke a leg, "would he go to a theologian, a doctor or a magician?" (1990, p. 345).

Let me respond to this line of reasoning by a return to critical and postmodernist theory. I do not want to overdraw the distinction between postmodernism and modernism and/or romanticism, as if my work does not have any roots in either view. When I am ill, I visit a doctor. When my father died, I wept for a man with whom I had a singularly unique relationship. Oftentimes, in the abstraction of our arguments, we end up painting academic dichotomies that hope to prove the brilliance of my argument and the foolishness of yours. We ought not create examples as either-or portraits, as in Ravitch's question, as if modern science holds answers and "primitive" magic is merely of anthropological interest. To assume that we have nothing to learn from the "magician" is as foolish as to overdraw a distinction in the opposite direction. "The advanced industrial nations of the world," comments Patrick Hill, "have cornered the market on neither wisdom nor science" (1991, p. 46). He goes on to point out how much we might learn from societies radically different from those based on Western thought.

Perhaps as with the Native American *berdache*, a blending of critical theory and postmodernism might offer us a third view. Critical theory works from the notion that collective change is possible. Indeed, a central aspect of critical theory is its desire to create the conditions whereby the citizenry are able to overthrow the oppressive aspects of society and seize power for themselves. Brian Fay is helpful in pointing out not only an underlying tenet of critical theory, but also a central disagreement with postmodernism:

The suffering of a group of people occurs in part because they have had inculcated into them an erroneous self-understanding, one embodied in and supporting a form of life which thwarts them. The aim of critical science is to stimulate these people to subject their lives and their social arrangements to rational scrutiny so that they can re-order their collective existence on the basis of the scientific understanding it provides. Critical science wishes its audience to reflect on the nature of its life, and to change those practices and policies which cannot be justified on the basis of this reflection (1987, p. 66).

Postmodernism's concern with such an aim is perhaps best summed up by Audre Lorde when she says, "The master's tools will never dismantle the master's house" (1984, p. 112). How is it possible to use "scientific understanding" and "rational scrutiny," the postmodernists ask, to change the logic on which those ideas have been built? The postmodern critique rejects the possibility of pluralist action that is based on foundations of romanticism or rational empiricism.

Critical theorists and postmodernists also have potential disagreements about the definition of identity. Although critical theory has rejected the idea of the autonomous human being that is capable of independent action, we do not learn from critical theory how people's lives might be radically reordered and reconceived in a manner different from rationalism's categories. We do not see how gender categories are brought into question or how an understanding of disease is transformed. Instead, we have the sense that critical theory's desire is to enable people to affirm their lives according to the fixed categories that already exist. In large part, critical theory's acceptance of these categories is a remnant of its modernist roots. After all, critical theory was originally conceived as a science and as a way to analyze society scientifically.

Postmodernism rejects categories. We uncover to how great an extent individual identity, self, is constrained by the mechanisms of power at work in society. Postmodernists point to Williams' work as an example of how a category such as gender has been created. A group that many point to as postmodern—the AIDS Coalition To Unleash Power (ACT-UP)—consistently fights the medical profession's desire to retain control over the cure for AIDS. Oftentimes, members of ACT-UP do not act "rationally"; they disrupt meetings, they shout slogans, and they engage in media events to bring attention to their cause. The work in which Williams and ACT-UP involve themselves is more than a simple attempt to develop a cultural relativism of sexuality or to effect the release of a drug for AIDS patients; their work involves fundamentally changing the categories—gay, straight, client, patient—that we currently use to think about ourselves.

Postmodernists argue that the inherent nature of power creates an inability for collective action in a manner with which we are familiar. We never "know" in a romantic or modern sense. Knowledge and identity are always partial and constructed, forever subject to multiple interpretations and reconfiguration. And since we cannot use rational discourse to deconstruct power, we are caught in something of a double bind in our attempt to act outside of the constructions of identity, for example, in order to understand identity.

Some postmodernists, of course, argue that our attempt ought not to be to try to understand identity; it is our focus on identity that has brought us the narrow definitions. The problem again revolves around the project's aims. "When postmodern arguments are extended," observes Kenneth Gergen, "we find it possible to replace an individualistic worldview—in which individual minds are critical to human functioning—with a relational reality" (1991, p. 242). In effect, postmodernism tries to de-objectify the definitions of self and identity and instead bring about a new vocabulary of being. Because I am uncomfortable with critical theory's overreliance on rationalist discourse, I am also dissatisfied with an approach that appears to have as an end in itself the creation of a new vocabulary.

The text that I develop here seeks to use these two ostensibly opposing points in the development of the concept of difference. I use postmodern insights about the fluid nature of categories such as identity, as well as an understanding of the constraints within which individuals operate. Critical theory picks up at this point insofar as it also acknowledges how individuals are both subjects and objects within discursive fields. But I extend critical theory's attempt at creating revolutionary change so that those oppressive structures that now silence us are overthrown, and we try to develop mutual dialogues of respect.

I neither see postmodernism's rejection of the "master's tools" nor critical theory's use of them as necessarily in opposition. I realize the inherent danger that is present by engaging in academic discourse—certainly a "key tool of the master"—but I also recognize the utility of critique. The problem, as I see it, is that critical theorists and postmodernists need to better define what they mean by political action.

Political/Apolitical

Often, we offhandedly acknowledge that our colleges and universities are decidedly less political than they were thirty years ago. Depending upon one's political persuasion, we look back upon such campus activities either fondly or with relief that the nightmare is over. We either bemoan the lack of activism on the part of this generation of students, or we applaud their desire to forego politics for education and training.

My problem with our nostalgic view of the 1960s concerns the manner in which we have defined the past and the implications for the present. We have equated political action with a specific act—the protest of the Vietnam War, in this instance. My quarrel is not with our memory of the sixties, but what our memory implies for the present. We remember overt campus protests and define those actions as political; we do not see such protests on college campuses today, and hence we decide that politics is absent from the campus. Such an assumption is wrongheaded if we take into account critical and postmodern notions of knowledge and power. The political economy of knowledge resides in academic institutions as much as in any other public institution. Scientific discourse both reproduces and regulates how we think about and act in the "real" world. Conversely, knowledge is also subject to constant political manipulation. As I made reference above, we disseminate, and hence regulate, knowledge through academic discourse that seeks to elevate and isolate forms of language from those whom we view as "unscientific."

I agree with Foucault, then, when he says, "Power is always there. One is never outside it; there are no margins for those who break with the system" (1980a, p. 141). To assume that politics existed on campus in the 1960s whereas it is now absent is a mistake; rather, a form of politics took place that now, for one reason or another, is not seen on campus, yet other forms of power still pervade the academy. From a critical perspective, to see campuses as political spheres in which power exists does not mean that one is inevitably trapped so that change is impossible. Rather, I conceptualize the institution as a culture with competing conceptions of reality.

The clearest example of these competing conceptions comes from the seemingly never-ending debate we are engaged in over the "academic canon." This debate, however shopworn the arguments may have become, is at the forefront in academe for several obvious—and a few hidden— reasons. The explosion of interdisciplinary courses and the corresponding creation of centers and departments offer evidence of how different groups have tried to engage the university with differing conceptions of reality. Those who say that Women's Studies or African American Studies are politicizing the academy are correct; they are doing so just as every other academic formulation of knowledge seeks to assert its own version of reality on the academy. Yet, however hopeful the opening up of the academy may have been to those of us concerned about multiculturalism, several residual problems exist that demand to be addressed.

In general, the debates over the canon have come primarily in the humanities and liberal arts, and to a certain extent, the social sciences. At most institutions, engineering and other professional schools, as well as the natural sciences, have not been involved in these arguments except in a peripheral manner. We learn from engineers, for example, how difficult a diversity-related requirement will be for students whose courseload is already full. We find out that the math department feels that its members do not have to deal with diversity in their curricula since their content concerns numbers and not ideas.

I offer this point to underscore how in many institutions vast portions of the faculty have absented themselves from the curricular debate because they have fixed definitions of knowledge. Pedagogy and curricula are uncoupled, and knowledge pertains to course content. The result is that many of us who are concerned about the nature of knowledge have been uniquely unsuccessful at transforming institutional cultures even though we have made dents in identifiable points such as how the institution defines general education. As I will discuss in Chapters 4, 5, and 6, however, the structure of the university often seems impervious to change even while we struggle to alter the nature of the curriculum.

Again, my point here is that those of us involved in academe are engaged in a political undertaking, and we ought not consider the ferment seen in the sixties as the only form of political action available to us. At the same time, we need to recognize the structure of the situation in which we are involved and work to change not simply a fact of knowledge, but also how the fact of knowledge is thought about and used, how it is related to other components, and who gains access to that knowledge. Such is the lesson from both critical theory and postmodernism, yet where the two differ is the public nature of political action. Critical theorists view action as essential, and postmodernists seemingly hold political activity as either useless or co-opting. In general, postmodernists also concur with Foucault's analysis:

The intellectuals have recently discovered . . . that the masses don't need them in order to know. They know perfectly well and much better than the intellectuals—and say it very well. But there is a system of power which checks, forbids, and invalidates this discourse and knowledge. . . . These very intellectuals are part of this system of power: the idea that they are agents of "consciousness" and discourse are part of this system (1973, p. 104).

From this perspective, academics—as well as other participants in institutions of power—are part of the embedded system of relations that silences "the masses." Thus, we are at a point in our history where we have lost public confidence in our ability to deal with the problems that confront us. On a national level no political leader or party engenders support. The American population believes that society will be worse for our children than it is for us. We now view problems such as inner-city crime, joblessness, homelessness, and unemployment as intractable and unsolvable. Perhaps we will be able to make minor changes here and there, but in general we no longer seem to believe in an American ideal that says we are all created equal and that we have the political and moral will to solve the problems that face us. Inequality is accepted passively, if not actively. Ninety percent of African Americans do not believe they will be treated fairly by our judicial system. Similarly, a majority of white Americans do not believe that integration is an achievable goal.

Obviously this is not the text to delve into an intellectual history of the last thirty years of the United States, but I am hard-pressed to disagree that we have good reasons for a loss of confidence in our leaders. I raise the point about public action because it is yet another distinction between those who subscribe to postmodernism and those who subscribe to critical theory. We have learned from postmodernism to distrust reality and reject definitions that try to invest a particular institutionalized discourse with knowledge and power. Our distrust and our cynicism of government or of the health-care system or of educational institutions is well deserved. We ought to applaud the extent to which common citizens question the answers provided to us. That we no longer accept a common language or the rationales that the government provide us are positive moments. Again, however, a critical theory needs to enter our discourse and enable us to do more than simply acknowledge that differences exist and that we cannot trust leaders, institutions, or even one another. Instead, we must engage in what I will describe as a cultural "politics of hope."

Hope/Nihilism

"As I looked for common passions," writes bell hooks, "sentiments shared by folks across race, class, gender, and sexual practice, I was struck by the depths of longing in many of us" (1990, p. 12). She goes on to write how this shared space and feeling "opens up the possibility of common ground where all these differences might meet and engage one another" (1990, p. 13). What hooks labels as "yearning," I define as "hope."

By hope I am not using a rhetorical device to speak about an unknown future as if we must accept our present conditions and await salvation or utopia. Instead, I use hope as a condition that offers meaning across differences. It is a concept that "is grounded in understanding our present conditions and delineating how we might change those conditions" (Tierney, forthcoming a). Hope has its roots in any number of different traditions, but it is most clearly articulated in recent critical ethnographic work. For me, hope has been expressed most clearly when I have shed the academic mantle and engaged in dialogue with people from diverse walks of life.

I hear a friend who is a faculty member speak of hope as he struggles with AIDS: "I know my situation is hopeless, that I don't have long. I don't hope for long-term recovery, but I haven't given up. Do you understand? It's more an acceptance of who I am. . . . I'm proud of who I am" (Tierney, forthcoming, a).

I also hear a lesbian college student speak of hope:

Every single day I hear offensive comments about gays and lesbians or women. I hear faculty make jokes in class. People will casually use words like "fag" or "queer," and no one will challenge them. But times do change. At National Coming Out Day this fall, over 500 people attended our rally on campus. And every single one of us was bursting with pride to be gay or to be in complete support of us. So you can't ignore us anymore. We're here to stay (Tierney, 1992a, p. 42).

And I hear a Native American student speak of his hopes for himself, his family, and his nephew and niece:

When I'm successful I want to raise the kids. I love them. I don't want them to face what I faced when I was a kid. My father was an alcoholic and I saw lots of bad things. It was tough growing up. I want a good job. Maybe a car. I want to show my family that I can do the best. . . . I suppose someday I'll get a college degree. I know one thing. I'll make it. I want to try to be something (Tierney, 1992b, p. 4).

To be sure, there are multiple interpretations that we might give to these comments. Perhaps the speakers are fooling themselves; in critical theory, we would use the term "false consciousness." One might critique the young man's "hopes," for in part they are typical adolescent desires—a car, a job. Another might question my friend's ability to speak of hope in a situation in which he has no control over his life. A third analysis might be that simply because a few students stood up at a "gay pride" day does not mean that political action has succeeded.

Another interpretation of these quotations and the idea of hope is that they have little to do either with theory or research. The modernist deals in science; hope is too much of a romantic notion to be applied to any theoretical understanding. A critical theorist grounded in modernism might point out that hope is a socially constructed category and does not enable us to understand how to overcome oppression and change society. A postmodernist views the idea of hope with suspicion, if not outright rejection. I have used the term as if the reader understands what I mean, as if there is a unifier called "hope." I also have offered examples from powerless individuals; are we to accept the hopes of the powerful as well?

As with many critiques, I am in partial agreement with the concerns I have outlined. There is a danger of romanticism in using "hope" as an analytic category. Hope does not tell us what to change—should we all desire cars?—or how to change. If we agree on what hope means, we may inevitably silence the hopes of others. But here's my dilemma: Postmodernism has taught us to reject organizing categories and the concept of progress or abstractions such as "truth." Modernism has shown us how we ought not blindly to have faith because of religious or natural imperatives. What, then, is the purpose of our lives? To what do we give meaning, other than immediate satisfaction? How do we exist in an otherwise sterile world? If we can answer these questions, we also might be able to answer the purpose of education, and how to organize our schools and colleges.

My concern with the postmodern critique is that it logically leads to inaction and nihilism insofar as concerted efforts are either futile or regressive. Yet a sense of futility is equally regressive. In effect, we have divorced our desires from our theoretical conceptions and in so doing we have paralyzed our ability to act. As hooks notes, "All too often our political desire for change is seen as separate from longings and passions that consume our time and energy in daily life. . . . Surely our desire for radical social change is intimately linked with the desire to experience pleasure, erotic fulfillment, and a host of other passions" (1990, p. 13). By invoking the idea of hope as a unifying concept, then, I am suggesting that we honor the words of individuals such as those I presented. But those words are neither decontextualized from the situations in which they present themselves nor are they divorced from a critical and postmodern analysis of society and community. Hence, I'm suggesting that we engage in a cultural politics of hope.

To be clear: dialogues of hope enable people to come together to define common and conflicting purposes, desires, and wants. Hope partially answers the questions about meaning, existence, and purpose, but dialogues of hope are not unifiers in a religious sense, in which a community defines its existence through specific beliefs. In a postmodern democratic community, conflict is inevitable and utopias will never be reached. And yet, having said that, I also am suggesting that some form of meaning must exist; otherwise we live in a passionless world at the least, and at the worst, we inhabit a nihilistic one where oppression goes unchecked and untrammeled.

My argument has its roots in the Deweyan philosophy (1966) in which cultural groupings exist within a society, but in which the culture also shares a range of common social concerns. We accept difference, we accept conflict, but we also search for commonalities. I am suggesting that through dialogues of hope we find these commonalities but that we utilize postmodernism and critical theory to recognize how power and authority shape and even thwart hope.

The concept of hope is helpful in providing meaning and a basis for action, but it neither tells us how to act, nor how to communicate across differences; it also suggests commonalities when none may be possible. Again, I am not suggesting that we lose the analytical work that has been done in critical theory and postmodernism—or in modernism, for that matter. Instead, I am trying to offer meaning and passion to a theoretical domain that we often find sterile. What remains is to suggest a more concrete framework for how we approach and organize institutional activity in educational institutions.

Difference/Agape

Earlier, I considered difference in terms of boundaries and border zones. Here, I extend that idea by considering how we organize around our differences so that we neither deny them nor make them insurmountable. As Lorde notes, "We do not have to become each other's unique experiences and insights in order to share what we have learned through our particular battles for survival" (1985, p. 8). Lorde's comment is in keeping with the basic points of this discussion: (1) there is possibility for change; (2) we must become involved in political work for change; (3) I will not renounce my individual identity in our engagement with one another; and (4) ultimately, there is the hope that we will be able to work together to build an equitable world.

The ideal of hope brings us to the central organizing topic of this book—agape. "Agape" is the Greek word made reference to in the New Testament and called upon by philosophers to speak of a specific form of love. In Greek we find three kinds of love—*eros*, or romantic love; *philia*, or brotherly love; and *agape*. Agape refers to selfless love. Martin Luther King, Jr. spoke of his life's work as one that involved agape. He wrote:

Agape is disinterested love. It is a love in which the individual seeks not his own good, but the good of his neighbor. Agape does not begin by discriminating between worthy and unworthy people, or any qualities people possess. It begins by loving others for their sakes. . . . It springs from the need of the other person. . . . It is love in action. Agape is love seeking to preserve and create community. It is insistence on community even when one seeks to break it. It is a willingness to sacrifice in the interest of mutuality and a willingness to go to any length to restore community (1958, p. 87).

An organization that works from the ideal of agape operates in a fundamentally different manner from other organizations. The underlying tenet here is that all life is interrelated. We are so connected with one another that if you are in pain, so am I. In this light, it is impossible to have a healthy institution when different individuals and constituencies are in pain. Gene Outka has pointed out that even when we disapprove of someone's ideas or behavior, "it still makes sense of regarding [the individual] as worthwhile and caring about what happens" (1972, p. 11). Such assumptions inevitably resituate how we think about organizational life in general and educational institutions in particular. For if we operate from a belief in agape, we must reorient our dealings with one another. The essence of this idea is that we are commanded to create community, to resist injustice, and to meet the needs of people.

As with the idea of "hope," I appreciate the theoretical, conceptual, and practical problems involved with arguing that agape is a useful concept for framing organizational life in higher education. In particular there are three central objections that might be raised. First, some will say that agape is yet another Eurocentric proposition for organizational life. Second, one might argue that we are not well served by utilizing an idea for "community" if we must use as examples communities from our recent past that have often been defined in terms of the exclusion of those of us who are different—women, people of color, the underclasses. And third, others will argue that we fall short by using agape if the term means nothing more than idealistic words that we cannot put into practice. How does agape help us answer the issues raised at the outset of this chapter about the problems of American higher education? How does agape help us find the revenue to refurbish buildings, increase financial aid, or employ faculty so class sizes may be smaller?

In large part, the remainder of this book is a response to these three concerns. I offer a provisional commentary here. Throughout Martin Luther King's writings, he invokes the life of Mahatma Gandhi, as evidence of someone involved in agape. "For Gandhi love was a potent instrument for social and collective transformation," King writes. "I came to feel that this was the only morally and practically sound method open to oppressed people in their struggle for freedom" (1958, p. 79). Agape, then, is not so much a term reserved for the exclusive use of biblical scholars, but rather, it is an analytical concept that awaits our interpretation and use.

Furthermore, postmodernism and critical theory ensure that we do not interpret agape as a consensual community based on similarity. Although some students of higher education might misinterpret agape as a synonym for what we have called a "collegial model," the collegial model is precisely what postmodernism has critiqued. The collegial model is an idea of like-minded faculty battling over abstract ideas with the assumption that "truth ultimately succeeds." The assumption is that consensus will be reached and that the nature of the community is real, concrete, and shared. The problem, of course, is that abstract notions of truth that obscure how we arrived at those definitions inevitably reward centric norms instead of bringing those norms into question. To engage in agape does not imply either that consensus will be, or ought to be, reached. We do not begin by assuming that one reality exists, but rather that there are multiple realities about issues and concerns that draw us into dialogue.

By assuming multiple realities, agape suggests that we accept one another's differences and work from those differences to build solidarity.

It is curious, perhaps, that I am suggesting that we build the idea of community around the concept of diversity, for communities generally suggest commonality. Such communities, however, have inevitably silenced those of us on the borders. Instead, we need to develop the notion of difference and engage in dialogues across border zones. Differences are confusing, even threatening, because we are forced to confront ideas and lives that may bring into question our own commonly held assumptions and beliefs, but I am suggesting that dialogues of difference also enable us to respond to the current challenges in education outlined at this chapter's start.

Given the complexity of the world that postsecondary institutions inhabit, it is foolhardy to assume that any work should provide a blueprint for administrative action. Nevertheless, I need to be more specific about how institutions might respond to the problems that confront us. In large part, how we define those problems relates both to the concept of agape, and to how we develop our answers. Patrick Hill is helpful here:

Marginalization will be perpetuated if new voices and perspectives are added while the priorities and core of the organization remain unchanged. Marginalization ends, and conversations of respect begin when the curriculum is reconceived to be unimplementable without the central participation of the currently excluded and marginalized (1991, p. 45).

Hill's comment responds to the concerns of agape I mentioned previously and establishes a direction for meaningful action. Educational communities that use agape as a central organizing concept are not institutions that define themselves hierarchically or in a manner that creates norms without bringing into question the borders. Instead, we investigate the structures and actions we take in terms of agape. It is inconceivable, for example, in an institution that works from the concept of agape, that different cultures within the institution would not be structurally engaged with one another.

As we currently function, however, the multiplicity of cultures that reside on our campuses are segmented and segregated in any number of ways. One group of students take Women's Studies courses, and no one else learns what takes place in those courses. A group of faculty work with other faculty in their disciplinary specialty and no one else. Administrators engage with one another and never deal with students. The staff function in a unitary world where they have no say over the actions of the institution. Each of these examples will be brought into question if we enact organizational agape.

As Patrick Hill comments, "Were a college or university truly committed to democratic pluralism, it would proceed to create conditions under which the representatives of different cultures *need* to have conversations of respect with each other in order to do their everyday teaching and research" (1991, p. 44). What Hill argues for is agape, insofar as all individuals are fundamentally connected to one another. Such a connectedness reorients our thinking about administration as well as how we develop the curricula. We reconsider what it means to be a faculty member or a staff member or a student; we develop different ways to decide what to do or what we think needs to be assessed. In effect, agape reorients the institution away from modernist concerns effectively and efficiently and toward a critical and postmodern engagement with empowerment.

VOICE, RESISTANCE, COMMUNITY: CRITICAL POSTMODERNISM

I spoke recently with a 40-year-old African American who has AIDS; a staff member at a large public university, he said:

I'm very reserved about my private life. You never know what will happen. Some people know, and others don't. I'm concerned about the one bigot out of ten who will discriminate. But the real problem is with the other nine people. There is a conspiracy of silence that forces gay people into the closet (Tierney, 1992a, p. 42).

I had two immediate thoughts when the individual made this comment. I first felt terribly sad. What kind of academic community have we built in which an individual is sick, dying, and is afraid to tell anyone for fear that he will be cast out of his community? Surely this is not a community focused on hope or agape.

My second thought was a flashback to a Native American college student I interviewed some years ago. Bruce Crow Flies High related a typical day at his university. In part, he said:

I'll go for a meal at lunchtime and eat by myself unless I see somebody from my high school. I don't mind it. One time a guy came over to my table and asked me if I had any friends. I could see the guys at his table must have put him up to it, because they were laughing. I told him I came here to get an education and that was most important. Most people leave me alone, and I leave them alone.

There's this one guy who always makes fun of my name—Crow Flies High. He'll joke about it. He doesn't mean anything by it. Some of the guys will laugh. At first he kind of made me ashamed of my name, but I spoke with someone else about it, and he said I shouldn't be ashamed, I should be proud (Tierney, 1992b, p. 74).

I had experienced a similar feeling of depression when this student related his story and after I had gathered additional information about the institution. He was a young man with dreams at a college that, if not denying those dreams, certainly did not support them.

To be sure, a number of possible responses arise from these quotations. A methodological rejoinder would be to ask if these sentiments are representative. Perhaps Bruce is just a loner. Perhaps if the individual with AIDS spoke with people, he would find support. Both of these comments are partially justified in the sense that as an author I have the obligation to contextualize data so that the reader gains a greater sense of the situation in which a speaker's comments are embedded.

The methodological comments also provoke another response from me, however. Those of us who are different probably do not need to ask if these quotations are representative. We live with feelings of exclusion and marginality daily. We carry our differences with us wherever we go. If I had presented a quotation from someone who had lived in North Dakota and she said, "It sure is cold in the winter," we would not ask questions of representativeness or generalizability. Instead, we would either know from our own experiences or from inferred experience that the speaker was right. Yet the heterosexual who has never thought about what it means to be lesbian, gay, or bisexual has no basis to understand the comments of the gay man with AIDS. The Caucasian who attends a campus where 95 percent of the student body is of the same race and who has never met a Native American does not know what it means to be a minority.

How do we create understandings across differences so that we are able to acknowledge and honor one another, rather than bring into question one another's legitimacy? It is incumbent on me as the author, then, to present these voices as fully and carefully as possible; at the same time, it is necessary for the reader or methodologist or administrator who does not understand these realities to try to come to terms with them. What I hope to do in this book is to present a way for us to develop this form of understanding.

And, of course, both of the quotations also demand attention from me as an individual; that is, my first response is not methodological but one of connection. I wanted to reach out to the man with AIDS and the Native American. One certainly does not need to be postmodern or critical to have a sense of compassion. But again, the theoretical frameworks we carry with us aid in understanding how to act. The liberal response to these individuals is to isolate these examples and deal with them. A support group for people with AIDS might be established. A Native American counseling center may be started. Without denying that such actions may be helpful, they do not change the fundamental relationships that lead to exclusion and difference. An organization founded on agape will deal with these comments in relation to the entire fabric of the university and consider how power is organized, defined, and used to muffle voices, and consequently, hope.

Postmodernists look to sentiments such as these as evidence of the necessity to destroy grand narratives of reality. I need to reiterate a point made earlier about how I have used the concept of postmodernism. Postmodern theory is not monolithic; indeed, it would be ironic if it were, insofar as yet another grand narrative would have been built. However, as I have critiqued postmodernism here, I have pointed out essential aspects of a European form of critique, for Continental postmodernism is better established and its points more finely made.

By calling for a relationship of critical theory and postmodernism, I am trying to develop what Henry Giroux has called "critical postmodernism" (1992). This form of postmodernism, notes Peter McLaren, "takes into account both the macropolitical level of structural organization and the micropolitical level of different and contradictory manifestations of oppression as a means of analyzing global relations of oppression" (forthcoming). Critical postmodernists see the individual as both object and subject in history, and locate action within a sociohistorical realm that gets acted out on a cultural terrain that is contested, redefined, and resisted. People are neither passive objects incapable of resistance, nor are they unconstrained individuals able to determine their own histories.

Furthermore, I am involved not merely in analysis, but in praxis. The work of praxis is not simply involvement in isolated examples here and there, but rather it is a strategic approach that runs throughout the fabric of the organization. Indeed, my purpose in this introductory chapter has been to develop the ideas of critical postmodernism so that we are able to use these constructs to analyze various aspects of postsecondary institutions. I have argued that a commitment to agape reorients the organization. I call upon the idea of hope in place of normalizing concepts such as "truth" because hope is dialogical. Hope offers purpose and meaning to our project, but it does so in a processual rather than deterministic manner. Individuals and groups engage one another to define what they mean by hope rather than accept the received wisdom of a community that has prearranged structures of knowledge that define truth. In developing these communities of dialogue, we accept that the possibility for change exists, but our goals are different from previous conceptions.

I assume that conflict will take place, and consequently I do not look for consensus. Critical postmodernists break boundaries and struggle to enter border zones with the realization that to do otherwise simply maintains traditional positions of power and authority. And the idea of identity is broken down with the recognition of the multiple and often conflicting identities we simultaneously hold as we span borders.

Culture, rather than a homogeneous entity, becomes a site of production and contestation not only over the goals in which we are engaged, but also over the processes we take to achieve those goals. Indeed, the processes exist in a dialectal relationship with goals so that the discourses we use to talk about our goals, and the relationships we establish to make decisions also determine what decisions are made. We cannot, for example, talk about evaluation and assessment of students and exclude students in the discussion; if we do so we cannot believe that our overall goal is a commitment to cultural democracy. We cannot create committees for organizational "downsizing" (i.e., firing employees) in which only senior administrators are involved and believe that we are engaged in organizational agape.

In what follows, I offer two case studies that further elaborate the ideas developed here. The next chapter delineates what might be a postsecondary education that is involved with dialogues of hope, respect, and agape. I define empowerment and continue the discussion about identity. In Chapter 3, I will talk yet again about identity, but as it concerns the ideology of silencing and the development of voice.

Chapter Two

Educational Mirrors: The Deep Springs Experience

"What does not change/is the will to change"
—Charles Olson, "The Kingfishers"

The data for this chapter derive from an extended visit to Deep Springs College in the fall of 1991. One may well wonder what, if anything, Deep Springs has to offer to the multitude of other colleges and universities in the United States. Deep Springs, founded in 1917 in the heart of the California desert, has but twenty-six students—all of them "men"—and never more than seven full-time faculty. The administration consists of the president; perhaps one of the faculty also will serve double duty as the academic dean.

Students come for two years and then in general depart for a traditional four-year college or university. Faculty stay no more than five years and often reside for a considerably shorter period. At present, the person who has the longest tenure at the college is the ranch manager, Geoff Pope, who has worked there for a decade as the overseer of the ranch that the students run.

The ranch, composed of three hundred cattle, some sheep, an alfalfa farm, and a large vegetable garden, accounts for one of the three central components of the Deep Springs experience. The students' formal academic program consists of liberal arts classes, all scheduled during morning hours. They spend the afternoon doing labor on the ranch. The students also govern the college in the sense that they hire the faculty, run the Admissions Committee for incoming students, and discipline students who run afoul of the student body's rules, such as those prohibiting the use of alcohol or drugs. Courses that are to be taught are approved by students, who frequently make suggestions about how an instructor might improve a syllabus. Most students and faculty say that the different kinds of classes that are offered, the work experiences that derive from the ranch, and the power that the students have in running the college make for a unique education different from what is found at any other collegiate institution in the country.

So, again, what might we learn from such a small, unique institution? I have two answers. First, I suggest that Deep Springs brings into sharp focus what is meant by the purpose of education. Not everyone needs to subscribe to the specific definition as Deep Springers describe it, but because the members of the college community have such a clear understanding of what they mean by education, it offers us the opportunity to reflect on how we might define education in our own institutions. Second, in part because of the college's size, but also because of the clarity in which their culture gets enacted, Deep Springs provides us a clear portrait of how change and innovation occur. Again, such a portrait allows for a degree of self-reflection about our own campus efforts that are aimed at educational innovation. In essence, I am suggesting that Deep Springs stands as a mirror for those of us concerned about the nature of postsecondary education for the twenty-first century.

Accordingly, this chapter has three parts. In the first section I will sketch Deep Springs in order to provide an understanding of the culture of the college. Then I will discuss the educational program by examining how Deep Springers define community, diversity, and intellectual freedom. Such a discussion underscores the unique mission with which Deep Springs operates. Finally, I will highlight the climate for experimentation at Deep Springs by elaborating on how assessment and communication take place and, in turn, by pointing out who functions as the organizational innovators.

I offer a caveat. Much of the recent writing on postmodernism has pointed out the role an author plays in the creation of a text. Although standard measures may be used to ensure that the data we call upon are valid, reliable, and trustworthy, ultimately these data exist as the author's interpretation of what the respondents said or did, an interpretation that obviously depends upon the author's values and biases. As is evident from Chapter 1, I am centrally concerned with developing postsecondary institutions in which diversity and multiculturalism are valued and honored. Thus, if my immediate objectives are to highlight (1) what Deep Springers mean by the purpose of education, and (2) how the organization's culture supports innovation and experimentation, my longer range goal here is to develop the ideas begun in the previous chapter. How might we as educators develop communities of difference where agape and hope are central characteristics?

By arguing that as educators we ought to be more forcefully concerned with developing communities of difference, I do not wish to suggest that Deep Springers also buy into that notion, or that the Deep Springs educational experience is a blueprint for such a community. Indeed, as I will discuss, Deep Springs has some significant points of divergence from what a community of difference might look like.

THE LANDSCAPE OF DEEP SPRINGS

If Deep Springs stands in contrast to other educational institutions, the same point also can be made with regard to the landscape one must pass through to reach the college. In general, one begins the last stage of the journey to Deep Springs in either Los Angeles or Las Vegas. One leaves, then, two of America's more glaring examples of urban environments where consumerism has run rampant and begins a daylong sojourn into the desert. The philosophy of Deep Springs is in many ways reflected in this desert that surrounds the college.

Everyone at Deep Springs can recite the history of the founding of the college. L. L. Nunn, a pioneer in the electrical power industry, was a self-made man. In the small mining town of Telluride, Colorado, Nunn built a power plant that used an AC generator—the first of its kind. For Nunn, the result was that he became rich and was therefore increasingly able to turn his interest—and money—toward education. From his tremendous wealth, he was able to found Deep Springs College.

Nunn selected the location for the college because of its isolation. A stone's throw from the Nevada border, the college lies in a remote valley in eastern California nestled in the Inyo and White Mountains. (Indeed, the surrounding countryside more accurately reflects what I think of as Nevada than California.) The ride from Las Vegas is a trip through desert terrain punctuated by an occasional town, a nuclear testing facility at Mercury, and the brothel known as the Cottontail Ranch (about 100 miles from Deep Springs.) Otherwise, the view is unobstructed; everywhere there is the open country of the desert.

Jackrabbits, coyotes, and birds are easy to see from the road, far easier to spot, in fact, than a neighboring car. From a pass about ten miles away, the college stands out in the summer sun because of the green expanse of the alfalfa fields, as well as the semicircle of houses that comprise the campus. Winding down the mountain path, one sees that Nunn's original vision has not changed very much. The solitude of the desert, to use Edward Abbey's (1971) phrase, is everywhere. No towns are in sight. Electrical wires do not crisscross the landscape bringing electricity to the local citizenry, for there are no local citizens other than those who reside at Deep Springs. The college has electricity, although there are no street lights. A few faculty have a VCR to watch an occasional movie, but otherwise, many of the accoutrements of modern society are absent. To be sure, students have CD players, computers, and the like, and the ranch is mechanized. Yet when a student uses the telephone and hears something akin to an echo chamber, he gets the unmistakable feeling that he has arrived in a remote area where a fax, express delivery services, and a host of other common conveniences will not be found.

The students are not allowed to leave the valley during the term. Faculty and staff occasionally venture to the nearby town, but it is an hour's drive away. Such isolation accentuates the intensity of college community living, for individuals need to depend on one another in a multitude of ways. Deep Springers like to point out that students must be responsible; if they neglect their chores and do not milk the cows, for example, there will be no milk. Just as important, if individuals do not communicate with one another, there will not be a sense of social support that is essential to the life of Deep Springs. A student cannot take off and go to town for a Friday night hamburger and movie. Two students cannot leave for a weekend of merriment elsewhere. Additionally, two students who dislike one another cannot split up and live on different sides of the campus; they must coexist in close proximity to one another. The community takes on a distinctly intense atmosphere.

In the valley, located along highway 266, a lone sign points to Deep Springs ranch. After the turnoff, the road goes for about a mile and then branches in two directions. To the right lies the lower campus, which entails the ranch and the houses of the staff. To the left lie the faculty and student quarters and the classrooms. On a quiet Sunday afternoon, my arrival at Deep Springs College reminded me more of visiting a specialized community such as that of the Amish or the Bruderhoff than it did of arriving at a more traditional college. Parking was no problem; indeed, few cars were in evidence. One fellow who was stretching and warming up for a run pointed me in the direction of the president's house. Because Deep Springs is so isolated—twenty-eight miles from the next town—I stayed at the college in a guest house that turns out to be next to the president's residence.

About a dozen buildings in a semicircle account for the campus. Nunn built most of the buildings and few have been renovated since the 1940s. There are five separate houses or residences for faculty, the president's house, and two guest cottages. The boardinghouse is where everyone eats, although at present it is being torn apart so that the kitchen can conform to the county's health standards. A misnamed "museum" houses a computer room, science lab, and classroom. The main building, in the center of the semicircle, is where the students live. It also contains a library, another guest room, a classroom, and an office for administration. The main building also has a large living room replete with a full assortment of couches and chairs that face in one direction. On Monday nights, students participate in "public speaking"—another of Nunn's ideas—to the college community. Students select the topics on which they will speak; on my visit I heard personal reflections about the college, political comments about the environment, a discussion about fishing rights for Native Americans, a commentary on the homeless, and a hilarious soliloquy about the music of Julio Iglesias.

Outside the living room is a large front porch, where a few students sit either reading by themselves or engaged in conversation. In the center of the buildings is a large grassy circle where a few students toss a frisbee back and forth. The "campus"—such as it is—is disorienting to the visitor. Where is the library? Where are the classroom buildings? The dorms? Indeed, where is everybody? Clearly, Deep Springs is not "everybody."

The student body is all men. Conversations have raged about whether women should be admitted, but no serious efforts have ever been made to change the college's charter so that the makeup of the student body might be altered. Consequently, the nature of the student body has stayed relatively stable over its seventy-five-year history. Deep Springers are quick to point out quite traditional indicators for the student body; they are in the top 2 percent of their high school classes; they regularly score 1400 on the SATs; more than half of the alumni have received doctorates; and fewer than 6 percent have not achieved a four-year degree. All of these facts are in keeping with Nunn's philosophy that Deep Springs should educate leaders, and in Nunn's time, he defined leadership by way of gender, that is, men.

Nunn also felt, however, that labor, self-governance, and living in community were important. All students work, and everyone participates in the life of the school. Clearly, working in the fields or living in the desert is probably not an activity that all students would desire for college. The uniqueness of Deep Springs, like all distinctive colleges, also defines the kind of students who will be attracted to such an education. And therein lies an initial paradox. It appears that a college in the desert that is as isolated as Deep Springs attracts *individuals*—people who do not desire traditional college support structures. Yet these Emersonian individuals must live in a *community* that is far more intense than any community found in traditional postsecondary institutions.

Meals are eaten communally, for example. Breakfast, lunch and dinner find faculty, students, and staff coming together. During my stay, I sensed a small degree of unspoken tension at these communal meals. When I asked others about the tension they concurred. Who sits with whom takes on importance. Do faculty only sit with other faculty? Who sits with the president and his wife? Do the ranch staff eat by themselves? The social dynamics of the meals underscore the tensions of living in community, for these individuals cannot escape one another. The teacher who gives a student a bad grade on an exam may find the student as a dinner companion or as the next person in the dinner line. The meals seem functional rather than social; individuals eat and leave. The meals are not long, involved gatherings where the community engages in philosophic debates or ritualistic celebrations; rather, discussion often turns on different aspects of the ranch. Some cattle were loose, for example, and someone needed to be up in the middle of the night to round them up or the watering system was not working correctly or an animal was to be slaughtered over the weekend.

The social dynamics of a meal also permeate the culture of the institution, for life in a community offers an intensity of experience. To highlight this intensity I turn to a discussion of education and the thoughts of different individuals within the Deep Springs community.

EDUCATION FOR EMPOWERMENT

To speak of education at Deep Springs is to speak of living in community. "There's a purpose to learning," commented one student. "I'm learning not just divorced facts and figures, but also about myself, about others." A second student added, "We're not faceless consumers here who buy a course and that's it. We're always in discussion." "Too much discussion," continued a third student. "This place can talk you to death." A fourth student elaborated:

Deep Springs can drain you. It can take everything you have, everything you're willing and able to give, and then it can take some more. There's the labor portion, feeding the animals or whatever, and then there's the classes, and the student government. You'd think out here in the desert we'd have time, but there's no time, no time to even sleep.

Others also mention how little sleep people have. En route to breakfast each morning, I saw a few students who had decided to sleep outside in their sleeping bags for one reason or another. One person's roommate had not gone to bed and studied in the room. Some students are up at dawn because they have to milk the cows. Others go to sleep at that time because they have been studying. Still others have had little sleep because they have been talking with one another. The business of the community centers around dialogue, but in a sense it is a curious dialogue, partitioned between formalized and rule-centered discourse and emotive and free-flowing conversation.

"Remember who comes here," explained one student. "Very bright, very verbal men." Another student pointed out, "We can be too tough on one another. We find weak points and go for it. Verbal jousting. The lightning wits of some people here can really level you." A third student commented, "People come here with hairline fractures in their character, and sometimes when they're hit with the Deep Springs hammer, they crack." A fourth student said: "You keep things inside. That's the only way to survive. Emotions are there and they aren't." And a fifth: "One has to live at a distance from one's emotional life to survive."

When I asked individuals if they had good friends here, lifelong friends, I received a variety of responses, "I didn't come here for that," said one fellow. "No, I don't think so," said another. "I disagree," said a third. "I dropped two of my friends off at the bus last week and I know when I saw them leave how I felt. They're real friends."

Another aspect of "friendship," "emotions," and the like pertains to issues of gender. All of the students are "men." Indeed, people seem to stress the word, "men," unlike at other schools where we might more commonly refer to eighteen- and nineteen-year-olds as "young men" or "boys." The only other times I have heard such constant reference to "men" are in outdated advertisements for the army in which they promised to "make a man of you." Perhaps part of the Deep Springs experience is also to "make men," but at present such a definition could not be more different from what the army once had in mind.

"We should talk about the 'guy stuff,'" said one man. Another student laughed and explained, "We talk about admitting women all the time and it's a big debate. One thing about us is that you can't always act like one of the guys." A third student continued, "We've been thinking about what it means for a man to have a feminine side. Perhaps nurturing. Like when someone's ill, somebody has to get his meal and take it to him, and it's going to be a man. That would probably be different if women were admitted." Another student offered an additional example, "The married faculty or the staff have kids, and we baby-sit them. We like to. I think it's different to find guys our age playing with five-year-olds." A faculty member concurred, "Playing with the children lets them put their guards down. And the kids love it. It's like having a bunch of caring, older brothers."

Still, issues of gender seem stilted and formalized. Other than when they played with the little children, the men seemed to act in some respects like stereotypical men. Physical distance was kept among one another. I saw no student touch another. Language, too, was formalized and often took on the tone of competition. Individuals pointed out that everyone wants to be good at his labor activities. "That's where you prove yourself," explained one individual.

By commenting in this manner, I am not suggesting that a community ought to be involved in constant emotional dialogue; yet we know from recent work by linguists such as Deborah Tannen (1990) and Shirley Brice Heath (1983) that different groups speak in different linguistic patterns and that gender is one of the key indicators of how those language patterns differ. The assumption at Deep Springs seems, however, to be that men need to consider what it means to be a man and that they best consider such an issue in isolation.

Indeed, the isolation of the community extends not only to the exclusion of women; people of color are also seriously underrepresented in the student body and faculty. "Students of color wouldn't want to come here," commented a student. "Students of color who qualify for Deep Springs will likely get a scholarship to Harvard or Stanford as well and they'll go there," said a second. Other students talked about the efforts that were currently underway in the admissions committee to insure that every possible avenue would be taken to find students of color. Again, my assumption is that the students' rationale may well be correct, and their efforts toward diversity appear to be well thought out and sincere. Nevertheless, although the situation is different because women are purposefully excluded, students learn about "difference" not by engaging with those who are different, but by turning inward and concentrating on their own individual lives and selves.

Individuals were sensitive when I mentioned that the community was homogeneous. "In some ways, we are. We don't have women here," said one student, "but there is a real diversity of opinion, amazing heterogeneity." A faculty member commented, "There is a heterogeneity of outlook.

You'll find a radical divergence of opinions. It's fundamental." Another faculty member asked, "How much heterogeneity can a small community tolerate? I think the real question is if we are producing students who only look at the world in one way, and the answer is very clear." The answer for that individual, as well as for most of the community, is that students leave Deep Springs with many different outlooks on the world.

A paradox is that the monastic life of Deep Springs is supposed to prepare students for an active life in the world. Such a belief follows in the most basic traditions of educational philosophy about what accounts for higher education. For traditionalists have long held the assumption that a postsecondary institution ought to be an island unto itself where individuals are able to reflect on the world in the rarefied atmosphere of a university. From this perspective, the work of an academic is not so much to engage in problem solving, but to develop his or her own stance toward life's great dilemmas.

The portrait of the disengaged intellectual who ponders philosophic issues is also one that has come under serious attack. Critics of many different political persuasions have argued that collegiate institutions ought to be more directly concerned with "real world" problems. One response has been that individuals need time away from the world in order to gain perspective before they "enter" the world. Such a view is partly in keeping with the educational assumptions of Deep Springs.

Nunn's philosophy was that students must lead lives dedicated to public service and in active support of the public good. The manner in which they learned a dedication to public service, obviously, was to attend Deep Springs. Yet unlike issues of gender or race, public responsibility is not simply learned by thinking about one's relation to such a concept, but by living the concept. That is, public service is a basic precept of the way in which Deep Springs conducts its daily life. The ethic of Deep Springs forces the individual to consider how he will repay society for the free education he has received. Individuals struggle to come to terms with how they will define service and duty to society once they have graduated from college. From this perspective, Deep Springs is the tool students use to develop their own definitions about their roles in life.

Faculty interact with students as much out of the classroom as in it; indeed, office hours are unnecessary in a college where the student can see the professor continually throughout the day and night. "When our porch light is off," commented a faculty member, "then they know that we need private time. Otherwise, students are free to drop by whenever they feel the need." A student pointed out, "I've learned the same amount in a traditional sense from the good and bad teachers. What makes teachers

good, however, is that they care, that they put out for the community."
Another individual added, "It's not just a job."

And as for students, one might continue, "It is not just study." In a
curriculum committee meeting that would continue until ten o'clock at
night, a group of students debated which courses should be offered during
the coming year. One student agreed to type course lists that would take
him the better part of several evenings. Another student needed to talk to
a faculty member about a course offering that would undoubtedly entail a
delicate conversation. A third student was not on the committee but he
attended the meeting because he was concerned about specific courses and
wanted to be involved in the dialogue. No one seemed to reject extra work;
rather everyone volunteered for tasks.

One of the primary leadership roles in the community is that of labor
commissioner; he is elected by his peers. This individual assigns the
manifold tasks that need to be done. Obviously some chores are more
desired than others. Working with the farmer in the fields has higher status
than washing pots and pans in the kitchen. A degree of fairness and an
understanding for individuals' strengths and weaknesses is a necessity for
the individual who assumes the position. A labor commissioner who gives
the best jobs only to his friends, or who gives an important task to someone
who is unable to do it, will create problems for the community. The
individual who holds this position explained his idea of the job:

In everyone's mind this position is close to the top of the hierarchy. It's important.
But I think this should be a humbling experience rather than something that exalts
you. In this job you have to learn how to work with people, rather than tell people
what to do. And it takes a lot of dialogue rather than threats.

A member of the ranch staff pointed out his view of his job: "I'm as
much a faculty member as anything else. These men come here and they
don't know anything about farming and ranching." Another ranch staffer
continued:

These guys are going to make mistakes out here. We give them responsibility and
they don't know how to do something and something goes wrong. Some of them
will own up to their mistakes and apologize, but they won't change. They'll keep
making the same mistake. The ones who seem more arrogant sometimes are the
ones who will follow through later, they'll quietly learn from their mistake and
not repeat it.

A faculty member agreed with the comments of the students and ranch
staff, "Responsibility is much greater here. People have got to come

through with their commitments, and there are a lot of them. You have to make sure that the cows don't get into the alfalfa and die. You also have to make sure that glasses are put out for lunch."

A student compared Deep Springs to other colleges, "Students elsewhere play at life as if it's a game, and the university just lets them do it. That's not true here." "I'm living responsibly," summed up one student. This sense of responsibility is yet another ingredient that adds to the intensity of the Deep Springs experience.

Three parameters of empowerment relate to Deep Springs. These parameters are my own, and they are based on a postmodern and critical theory of education that concerns itself with building organizational agape.

Understanding the "Other"

As for the first point, recent social theory has taught us that there is not one reality in which all individuals reside, but multiple realities that are socially constructed and continually redefined. An educational process concerned with empowerment needs to engage students so that they are able to learn about themselves by coming to terms with the "Other," with those who may be quite different. The point is neither to mindlessly develop a hyperrelativism through which one group's beliefs are as good as another's, nor to engage in "a patronizing notion of understanding the Other, but a sense of how the self is implicated in the construction of Otherness" (Giroux, 1990, p. 31). Traditional notions of education assume that knowledge is more static and, correspondingly, that moral absolutes exist. As I noted in Chapter 1, a critical postmodern stance investigates how knowledge gets created and what the relationship of power is to the categories and discourse of knowledge. We discover, then, not constant, unchanging truths that are handed down Moses-like generation to generation, but rather we seek to interpret identities and voices that have been silenced and dispossessed.

Deep Springs attempts this activity, and it does so in an odd fashion. The students at Deep Springs learn about the Other by their absence. Students appear to struggle with issues of sexuality, for example, not in mutual dialogue between men and women, but in conversations among men. From the perspective advanced here, Deep Springs is partially successful in its desire to understand the Other. If conversations are any indication of what is important to a community, then the Deep Springs experience is crucially concerned with issues such as gender, class, and race. Such discussions occur frequently in formal settings such as classes and informally among students and faculty in countless other settings. In that light, the educational program is one example of the struggle for understanding other realities. A Deep Springs education encourages students to investigate claims of knowledge and truth in reference to the students' own lives and not as moral absolutes. As I will elaborate, because students must deal with a heterogeneity of ideas in their community, they also actively grapple with understanding them. How knowledge is constructed and defined is of concern at Deep Springs. Thus, simply because the question has been raised, we see that Deep Springs is involved in an educational process that struggles to understand the Other.

Yet because of the homogeneity of the individuals' backgrounds, the processes in which they encounter the Other are remarkably similar. How would the Deep Springs experience be different if only women were involved? How would it differ if the student body were all African American? I am suggesting that the manner in which educational realities and communities are constructed and played out will have remarkable variability depending upon the makeup of those individuals involved. And to the extent that Deep Springs is unable to diversify its student body, they will only be partially successful in understanding. By studying issues such as race and gender abstractly, the students of Deep Springs avoid having to deal with the voices and ideas of women and people of color. Ultimately, a community of difference must be a community that not only studies difference but also is different in terms of culturally defined phenomena such as gender, class, race, and sexual orientation.

At most institutions with which I am familiar, discussions about issues such as class, race, or gender are absent (Tierney, 1989; Tierney, 1992b). We neither find such conversations inside or outside of the classroom. Reflecting the makeup of collegiate America, the vast majority of these institutions are coeducational. Although all of the institutions are racially integrated to a greater or lesser degree, what I have found is a remarkable lack of community-wide "dialogues of respect and difference." Deep Springs undertakes such dialogues in a unidirectional manner. Individuals strive to understand differences by reflecting on their own lives. Although such dialogues are an improvement over no dialogues at all, the lack of engagement with women and people of color appears to stifle the kind of empowering educational program that a critical postmodern project seeks.

Individuals in Community

Perhaps the second point, the idea of individuals functioning within a community, is Deep Springs' greatest strength. Even before students arrive, by way of the application process they are socialized to the fact that this college is theirs to make of it what they will. The seeming contradiction of being an individual and living in a community is enacted on a daily basis. To be sure, there are challenges and hurdles that are not always overcome. One might hope for greater interaction with one another in terms of emotional support, for example. Yet in contrast to their detached engagement with the Other, Deep Springs students have developed a life in which each individual is forced to come to terms with the meaning of citizenship, social responsibility, and intellectual freedom. These encounters actively define the immediate community and presumably impact on an individual's view of how he should lead his life after Deep Springs. Unlike their abstract study of the Other, students must actively decide for themselves how they define social responsibility or good citizenship.

The Discourse of Democracy

In large part because of the first two points discussed, students have control over their lives and the community. As with other intentional communities, most individuals exhibit a remarkable concern for virtually all aspects of communal life. Again, to an outsider, the degree to which the students control the curriculum, for example, stands in sharp distinction to other colleges. Where else would it be considered normal procedure for a student-run committee to ask an individual with a Ph.D. what credentials he/she has to teach a particular course? What such control has done is to provide students with the tools to take charge not simply of a syllabus but of their lives.

Conflict in a democracy is inevitable and necessary, and one finds such conflict at Deep Springs. Individuals disagree, and tension exists between the students and administration, as well as between and within other groups. Unlike many other postsecondary institutions, however, Deep Springs—perhaps because of its geographic isolation and resulting reliance on one another—cannot paper over conflict. In some form, it must be resolved, and in general that form is the dialogue and debate that is central to democratic processes.

Each of these points—(1) understanding the Other, (2) individuals in community, and (3) the discourse of democracy— embodies what I mean by empowerment. A student who has not engaged in understanding the Other or has not considered what it means to be both an individual and a member of a community or has not actively participated as a member of a democracy will not have encountered an education concerned with empowerment.

When we think of the vast fabric of American higher education and the manifold ways in which teaching and learning are delivered, we find few institutions that have operationalized these parameters in a clearer way than Deep Springs. One strength of postsecondary education in the United States, it has been said, is the diversity of our delivery system. I am not suggesting that all postsecondary institutions must adopt the Deep Springs model, but as I noted at the outset of this chapter, I find that the clarity of their approach enables us to be more reflective about the educational programs at our own institutions; Deep Springs holds up a mirror for us.

One other remarkable point about Deep Springs is that this "experiment" has been in existence for seventy-five years. Whereas most other innovative programming has either withered and died, such as Black Mountain College (Duberman, 1972), or regressed to the academic norm such as at the University of California–Santa Cruz, Deep Springs has remained stable in its ability to sustain a state of constant change. At first glance, it appears oxymoronic to claim that an institution's stability is in its ability to change. Accordingly, we now turn to a discussion of how Deep Springs' unique sense of identity has been maintained.

CREATING A CULTURE OF STABILITY AND CHANGE

"Our history is oral," points out one individual. Another person adds, "Stories get passed from one group to another about what Deep Springs is about." When I comment to one individual that it seems that the college does not have many overt rituals or ceremonies, he disagrees, "We don't have rituals like graduation, if that's what you mean. Our rituals occur in the rhythm of the day, in the labor, in the meals. You know that breakfast is at a particular time, that in the summer you will work in the fields. Those are our daily patterns." His point is that although Deep Springs does not have any ceremonies passed from generation to generation, the college survives by way of what Erving Goffman has called, "interaction rituals" (1967). These rituals frame how individuals and the community communicate with one another, and these rituals are passed on to each incoming group.

As noted previously, no one stays at Deep Springs for long periods. The students leave within two years; the faculty and administration stay five years at the most. One false assumption that might be made is that such constant comings and goings create a climate of instability and the potential for a weak culture that is void of a sense of identity. That is, the definition of a "distinctive college"—to use Burton Clark's (1970) phrase—stands in stark contrast to the culture of Deep Springs. Distinctive colleges, such as Reed College or Swarthmore College, have individuals who embody the institution. It is not uncommon to find faculty members who have lived and worked at the distinctive institution for most of their adult lives; rather than being tied to the culture of their discipline, they are oriented to the culture of the institution. The institution often is led by a strong-willed person who provides a sense of direction and purpose. And the college has quite specific mechanisms for socializing new members and a wealth of rituals and ceremonies that bring the community together periodically throughout an academic year.

Deep Springs has none of these attributes. Faculty think of themselves in terms of their disciplines, and indeed they must, for they will be at the college for less than half a decade. Administrators are often irrelevant; when individuals speak about the history of the institution, no one brings up famous names of any of the college's presidents who have made a lasting impact in a manner akin to presidents at other institutions. Indeed, if anything, individuals point out a president in the 1950s who tried to provide direction and was apparently resisted. Socialization occurs indirectly. Rituals and ceremonies are nonexistent, except in the manner described.

Any student of higher education or organizational culture, however, will immediately identify Deep Springs as an institution with a distinctive culture. Curiously, the constant turnover at Deep Springs has created a climate of identity and stability. I am suggesting that Deep Springs is a culture in which the members identify with the college not because tribal elders exist who pass along the "truths," but rather because the institution demands that individuals seize responsibility for their college and their education as soon as they arrive.

I was surprised, for example, during my stay at Deep Springs when I saw so many students doing work that seemed boring but nonetheless essential. One student dug a ditch for an underground watering system. Another student washed the dishes after meals, and still another was up at two in the morning to help the ranch staff move that cow off the road. Students at other colleges also work in kitchens to earn money, but Deep Springs students receive no income for their labor. At the vast majority of institutions, to ask students to undertake tasks such as rounding up cows in the middle of the night or digging a ditch would be met with astonishment. If the Deep Springs students did not perform these tasks, the college could not function, and more fundamentally, the college would no longer be Deep Springs.

Because Deep Springs is a cultural anomaly, it is also different with regard to the manner in which it conducts assessments. As I will discuss in Chapter 4, during the last decade a considerable literature has arisen that calls for student-oriented outcomes and assessment of student learning. The argument has been made that specific goals must be reached, and, as consumers, students have the right to know specific indicators that an institution uses to measure quality. In general, the assessment movement in the United States is a dialogue not about the processes of educational life, but about the goals.

At Deep Springs, however, assessment is a process as much as a goal. The intense introspection of the participants in the institution demands an ongoing assessment of what is being learned. One student has commented in a paper about the college, "We think about what we are doing so much, it makes us sick. We all start this process practically the day we arrive. By now I am well accustomed to looking critically at what I and the community as a whole are doing" (Glenn, 1991, p. 7). Students assess what occurs at Deep Springs from a variety of perspectives, including the manner in which student learning takes place or what would normally be called "out-of-class" learning experiences.

Another unique aspect of assessment at Deep Springs concerns those who have a substantial role in assessment—the students. As noted at greater length in Chapter 4, most of the literature assumes that "experts" will conduct and analyze the outcomes and assessment mechanisms of an organization. Implicitly, the literature assumes that experts are older adults, often with doctorates, and often working in an institutional research office. While student opinions might be used to gauge a particular aspect of the process, students are not in charge of the assessment. At Deep Springs, assessment is a constant, ongoing process that lies in the hands of those who have the most to gain—the students.

I am suggesting that the climate for innovation and change at Deep Springs has been maintained in large part because of an educational philosophy that calls for the immediate ownership of the institution by the student body. Assessment is not something done by, or for, an external organization. The definition of "what this place is about" is also something that undergoes constant, active discussion, debate, and redefinition.

I ought not overlook certain structural characteristics that also play a role in the educational climate and culture at Deep Springs. The size of the college allows introspection and communication to occur in a manner that would be distinctly difficult to reproduce at a large, urban institution. Indeed, several students point out to me that it is the college's isolation and desert location that allow for such a unique culture.

And, too, the alumni and board of trustees offer an invisible hand of continuity. Although the trustees meet only twice a year, their presence is constantly discussed. They seem to guide the college in a manner that is remarkably unobtrusive. Perhaps because most of the board members are former students of the college, they view themselves not as activist board members who direct the policies of the institution, but rather as individuals who insure that the basic precepts of the college are maintained. Obviously, student voice and governance are among those sacred rules, a fact that inevitably lessens the traditional authority of a board of trustees.

Finally, the students also arrive at the college with personal attributes ideally suited to the college culture. These students are, in general, individuals who will excel wherever they attend school. They are in the top 2 percent of their high school classes; their SAT scores are phenomenal; most of them have offers to attend Ivy League schools. Some observers might say that with students such as these assessment is not important since we know these students will do well in any college. Other individuals might comment that for students who are not so gifted academically, milking cows will be a tremendous waste of time. Still others will comment that the college is not designed to meet the needs of today's students—many of whom attend school part-time or cannot afford the luxury of two years in the desert. Such criticism returns us to the question I posed at the beginning of the chapter: If we use Deep Springs not as a model but as a mirror, what might we learn for academe in general?

CONCLUSION

I began this chapter with a quotation from the poet Charles Olson, the last president of Black Mountain College. Olson's (1966) statement—"What does not change/is the will to change"—accurately reflects the successful dualism of stability and change inherent at Deep Springs. The school is able to foster a climate for change by maintaining a culture in which the participants are actively involved in the creation of their mutual destinies. The institutional participants judge whether they are achieving their goals not in a formalized manner set up to please an accreditation body or an institutional research office, but in an ongoing, informal way that occurs through dialogue with one another.

Deep Springs has created an organizational culture based on a philosophy of educational empowerment that permeates the daily actions of the institution. As educators, if we want students to seize control of their lives, what the Deep Springs experience teaches us is that students must be actively involved in learning more than simply by speaking in a class or participating in an out-of-class activity. We must create conditions under which students are able to struggle in abstract and practical ways with questions about what it means to live and work in the democratic sphere in the late twentieth century. From this perspective, to read in a class *about* philosophic values but not engage those values in one's life is a mistake. Similarly, to study about other people but not to live and work with individuals and groups different from ourselves also seems a mistake.

The assumption here is that the best preparation for democratic participation is to participate in democracy. Of necessity, these educational conditions must enable students to come to terms with who they are by investigating other realities, participating in communal life, and coming to terms with what democracy actually means. Knowledge, then, is not something abstract and universal that is delivered by faculty and absorbed by students, but instead it is something that is tangible, momentary, and contextual that is constructed in concert with others. Teachers are not authorities who lecture; they are coparticipants in a learning experience.

Undoubtedly, not all students will resonate to a collegiate life that is circumscribed by cattle and desert solitude. I am not suggesting such an approach. Rather, I am arguing that at a time when student voices and authority have been muffled, we need to think of creative ways to engage those voices more fully. We are currently at a time when much debate takes place about whether we should have national assessment criteria for postsecondary education; I am suggesting that rather than develop minimalist standards, we need to foster and to encourage learning communities in our postsecondary institutions that give students greater direction over their lives. Thus, the mirror of Deep Springs ought not force us to look and think like a college in the desert, but rather should enable us to see ourselves more clearly so that we are all able to participate more fully as democratic citizens of the twenty-first century.

Chapter Three

Public Roles, Private Lives:
Gay Faculty in Academe

"Woe to him who doesn't know how to wear his mask."
—Luigi Pirandello, *Henry IV*

As with the story of Deep Springs College that has but twenty-six students, one might initially ask what we have to learn from the data I use in this chapter—interviews with four gay faculty members at one university. Aside from standard methodological concerns pertaining to generalizability, we also might wonder about what gay faculty have to tell us that will improve the climate in higher education and attend to the pressing concerns that I outlined in the introduction to Chapter 1. What do the personal experiences of gay faculty have to do with making postsecondary institutions more responsive to the demands of the twenty-first century? From a traditional perspective, the answer to such a question is that such stories probably have quite little to do with improving colleges and universities. Not surprisingly, I argue otherwise.

In what follows, I extend the discussion of critical postmodernism and organizational agape by focusing on how we conceive of identity and difference. As I will explain, at this moment there is probably no group more appropriate to use in a discussion of identity and difference than gay, lesbian, and bisexual people. Through an analysis of the comments of four faculty and the contextualization of their words, we find startling challenges about traditional notions of identity and difference. And yet, we have virtually no research pertaining to the lives of gay, lesbian, and bisexual individuals in academe. One might be curious as to why a vacuum exists

and what it portends for our definition of community. How is it possible
to construct a community based on difference if we do not enable those
who are different to speak?

And when they speak, with which voice will their stories be told, for
we all hold multiple narrative voices. Jane Tompkins writes that she has
two voices that "exist separately but not apart. One writes for professional
journals; the other in diaries, late at night" (1987, p. 169). Tompkins goes
on to point out how a public/private distinction exists among academics
where what they theorize in their public lives and what they do in their
private lives is supposedly unrelated. She continues:

The dichotomy drawn here is false—and not false. I mean in reality there's no
split. It's the same person who feels and who discourses about epistemology. The
problem is that you can't talk about your private life in the course of doing your
professional work. You have to pretend that epistemology has nothing to do with
your life, that it's more exalted, more important, because it (supposedly)
transcends the merely personal. Well, I'm tired of the conventions that keep
discussions of epistemology, or James Joyce, segregated from meditations on
what is happening outside my window or inside my heart (1987, p. 169).

Even more so, through the interviews of the gay faculty presented here
we come to terms with the implications of the public/private distinction
for building a community of difference. On the one hand, we discover that
there are quite good reasons why individuals keep their private lives
private. On the other hand, we see how the desire to exclude one's personal
feelings and emotions from research efforts inevitably privileges norms
based on heterosexual, white, male values (Jaggar, 1989). I am suggesting
that because of the culture and ideology currently at work in academe there
are quite good reasons why individuals keep quiet about their sexual
orientation, but in doing so, we continue to reinforce norms that deny hope
and muffle voices.

This chapter has three parts. In the first section I contextualize the
"ideology of silencing" (Friend, 1992) by first discussing the general
context of homophobia and heterosexism and locating these concepts
within academe's borders. I then offer a series of interviews with faculty
at a public university. I examine their discourse about how they perceive
their public roles as faculty members and how these roles often conflict
with their private lives as gay men. The final section unites the ideology
of silencing with the interviews through an analysis of how we might
reformulate what we mean by identity and difference.

My intent here is to focus on identity and difference so that we might
come to terms with the discontinuities we face on a daily basis in our

colleges and universities. Once we understand these differences and how we have marginalized some individuals and privileged others, we may be able to develop a sense of how we engage in organizational agape so that the wearing of masks becomes unnecessary and we are then able to develop specific recommendations.

THE IDEOLOGY OF SILENCING

The Power of the Norm: Heterosexism and Homophobia

"When you know that what you say is likely to provoke a negative reaction, you hide. And that's what has happened to us historically," commented a young professor at Normal State University (a pseudonym), and this statement reflects a gay, lesbian, and bisexual history of oppression and invisibility (Katz, 1976).

In the twentieth century, for example, if we read a work such as *The Pink Triangle* (Plant, 1986), we learn about the fate of gays and lesbians in specific contexts such as Nazi Germany. Gay and lesbian prisoners were confined to death camps where, forced to wear pink and black triangles, they constituted the lowest rung in the camp hierarchy and were systematically exterminated. Closer to home, the United States military has allowed lesbian and gay people to serve and to die for this country during wartime, but when they return home, they are given dishonorable discharges because of their sexual orientation (Berube, 1990). Gregory Herek (1989) and Anthony D'Augelli (1989) have documented instances of lesbian, bisexual and gay people who were victims of anti–gay/lesbian violence. Given such a climate, lesbian, gay and bisexual people have hesitated in "coming out"—the process of revealing one's sexual orientation. If someone does so, he or she is likely to face discrimination of one form or another.

The twin concepts of heterosexism and homophobia help shape the discrimination faced by lesbian and gay people in general, and specifically in colleges and universities. Audre Lorde has defined heterosexism as "a belief in the inherent superiority of one pattern of loving over all others and thereby the right to dominance" (1985, p. 3). The assumption that everyone is, or should be, heterosexual enables homophobia to exist. Homophobia is the fear and hatred of homosexuality in oneself and others (Friend, 1992). These related concepts feed off one another. The assumption that everyone is "straight" creates the idea that anyone who is not should be looked upon and treated as aberrant; the fear of homosexuality reinforces the idea that everyone should be heterosexual.

As we shall see, these concepts have constructed lesbian and gay identities at Normal State University by way of the institution's ideology and culture. In doing so, the power of the "norm"—heterosexuality—has maintained a pervasive hold on defining the boundaries of what constitutes acceptable or deviant behavior. In turn, individuals strive toward conformity rather than empowerment.

Culture and Ideology

Colleges and universities operate in cultural spheres rooted in an ideological framework (Tierney, 1991). For example, the institution of this study, Normal State University, has a culture that permeates the way the organization's participants act. Henry Giroux has defined culture as "a complex of traditions, institutions, and formations situated within a social sphere of contestation and struggle, a sphere rooted in a complex of power relations that influence and condition lived experiences without dictating their results" (1983, p. 164). Institutional culture both defines and is defined by the organizational actors. Cultures of colleges and universities sustain and reframe institutional ideologies. (By *ideology*, I mean the set of basic beliefs that orients the culture of the organization.)

One might question whether an institution's ideology or culture has any relation to the lives of lesbians and gays. How, one wonders, is an individual's sexual orientation influenced by an organization's culture? Does ideology enter into any relational aspects of sexual identity? The answers to those questions go to the heart of this chapter's argument. I am suggesting that we cannot talk about institutional diversity divorced from power-laden concepts such as culture and ideology. As Giroux has noted, "Questions of Otherness are generally fashioned in the discourse of multicultural education, which in its varied forms and approaches generally fails to conceptualize issues of race and ethnicity [and sexual orientation] as part of the wider discourse of power and powerlessness" (1990, p. 10). In other words, the assumption is that one simply needs to change people's attitudes and diversify the makeup of academe's different constituencies; once that is done, the thinking goes, the institution will have become more diverse.

Michel Foucault is helpful to counter that idea: "The problem is not changing people's consciousness—or what's in their heads—but the political, economic, institutional regime of the production of truth" (1980a, p. 133). We move, then, from an individualist stance, which assumes that whatneeds to change are individual identities, to a theoretical perspective, which assumes that how power is situated and defined in large part determines the parameters of diversity. The challenge is to uncover those ideological norms in an organization's culture that silence and make invisible gay and lesbian lives.

Contextualizing Silence: Normal State University

Normal State is a traditional, large public university that has been in existence for over 100 years. An analysis of all of Normal State's diversity-related documents reveals that lesbians and gays are virtually non-existent in the organization's explicit culture. The alumni office has never considered creating a lesbian and gay alumni network. The official communication vehicles of the university, such as the newspaper or the Office of Public Affairs, have never discussed gay and lesbian issues. Documents that call for awards for faculty or staff have never mentioned that work in issues pertaining to sexual orientation account for anything. Student course evaluations ignore categories that try to gauge whether an instructor is homophobic or gay-supportive. Normal State's library has no person assigned to lesbian, gay and bisexual scholarship.

The power of the norm also is reinforced in an organization's culture through a structure that develops policies that privilege some and make others invisible. At Normal State, no policies exist that pertain to lesbians, gays and bisexuals. When this study was undertaken, the university did not have a sexual orientation clause that prohibited discrimination, so lesbians, gays and bisexuals were not even protected from harassment and job discrimination. Individuals who are married to a Normal State employee, however, are allowed certain privileges and services, from the mundane—use of the swimming pool, for instance—to the important—health care. None of these privileges exist for lesbian and gay couples; the university does not recognize that individuals may be in committed relationships if they are not married.

Further, any workplace has a myriad of discursive symbols that convey many of the beliefs and assumptions of the community. The use of in-group language and numerous other communicative activities promote a culture that purportedly unites the community. Yet symbols also have the potential to exclude some members. A norm, for example, at Normal State is to find any number of heterosexual faculty and staff who have pictures of their spouses and families on the wall. Informal discussions often revolve around what an individual and his or her spouse do on vacation or over the weekend. Office parties involve the spouses of faculty and staff so that everyone has a chance to know one another. In essence, each of these and countless other examples are symbols that create a bonding within the Normal State community. Some will argue that such socialization practices also help to create a comfortable work climate that enables individuals to work effectively with one another.

Yet each of the symbols points out how bisexuals, lesbians, and gays are excluded. Gay, lesbian, and bisexual persons cannot call upon similar symbols for the simple reason that if they do, they face discrimination or contempt from their colleagues. As we shall see, a picture of one's partner on an office wall is likely to engender disapproval, which in turn may compromise an individual's position in an office, or even his or her employment. Thus, attitudes about gay, lesbian, and bisexual individuals are either negative or absent. The symbolic life of the community reinforces the culture of those who are in the mainstream—heterosexuals.

What follows are data developed from a research project that involved interviews with twenty-four gay and lesbian faculty over the course of an academic year. Three other researchers and I formed a team that conducted these interviews. Each interviewer worked from the same protocol; the interviews lasted for a minimum of one hour, and some individuals were reinterviewed a second and third time. I present here information from four of the interviews.

We first hear the faculty provide their own interpretations of the culture and ideology of Normal State. The faculty are gay men who range from 33 to 45 years old; three are assistant professors and one is a full professor. I have held gender constant not in an essentialist manner as if all men and women think alike, but in the realization that gay men and lesbians face fundamentally different problems and perceptions of their worlds. (For an analysis of lesbian faculty, see Bensimon, 1991.) Similarly, I have concentrated on faculty rather than including staff members so that we might gain a better understanding of the manifold challenges faced by one particular constituency within academe's borders.

SILENCED LIVES

"Being gay is a part of my self that I've learned to hide in order to survive," commented Don, an assistant professor in the humanities. Jack, also an assistant professor, agreed:

You come out of one closet and go into another. I really struggle in every class I teach whether to come out to my class. I know students who say, "I don't know anyone who's gay." They only know gays as sick psychopaths in the movies—sad, pathetic, creatures. I feel it incumbent on me to be a role model. But I don't know if I want it to be an issue. But it is an issue.

The "issue" of being gay has played a role in all of the interviewees' lives. Each individual has hesitated in "coming out"—a process of telling others about their sexual orientation. By and large, they have stayed "in the closet." Even Bruce, a full professor, pointed out that he never discusses his private life with his colleagues: "I think some in my department know that I'm gay, but I would never discuss it. I tell people who I'm comfortable telling, who can handle it. I've told one person so far."

Don, Jack, and Bruce are worried about how their colleagues will treat them if the private fact of being gay becomes public. Robert, another assistant professor, faces an additional concern; he has AIDS. "Of course I'm worried, sensitive to what people will think: 'God, this person's a faggot,' they'll say. And then with AIDS, I'll have to face all the stigma that goes with it. So I've been quiet. I don't want people to know about me."

Although similarities exist as to why each individual hides his life, the form their secret takes differs from individual to individual. Don is the most open of the four faculty, yet he also experiences the most discomfort at being "out." "Some people in my department know I'm gay because I've told them," related Don. "And I suppose others have found out. People may not care if you're gay as long as you're not visible, as long as you're closeted." He continued by relating a story about his birthday:

There's a gay bar in town—the only gay space in this town—and it is directly across the street from campus. You have to make a statement when you go in there. You don't know the consequences if someone sees you going in—a student, or your department chair, or someone on the promotion and tenure committee.

I remember when Wendy (a colleague and friend) took me for a drink on my birthday. We started to go into Friendly's (the bar) and we saw our department head and a very conservative colleague sitting in a restaurant nearby. We had to make a choice. They might see us going in. . . . These are the kinds of things you think about when you're gay.

To varying degrees, Don's concern was echoed by the others. Bruce will not go into Friendly's because he does not want to have his students see him enter a gay bar. "It's just too public. Right there across from campus," he said. Jack also is concerned about his students, but not about if they see him going into a bar. "I feel it incumbent on me to be a role model," he said, "but I'm worried what they will think."

Of the four faculty, Robert is the only one who is also a person of color. Because of his race, Robert added a particular twist to his concern: "As a [person of color] I always have tried to be a role model for the younger ones. Young [minority] college students look up to me. Gay people need that too, I did when I was growing up, but I'm worried about coming out and facing hostility, especially now that I have AIDS. So when I've been in the hospital I haven't let anyone know."

The individuals' concerns about student responses to their sexual identity were twofold. On the one hand, Robert and Jack perceived that the function of a faculty member, in part, was to serve as a role model to students. On the other hand, the four faculty members were concerned that if students found out that a professor was gay, the students might use that information to an individual's detriment. Jack, for example, had recently applied for jobs at other institutions. "People ask for my course evaluations," he explained. "All you need is a vocal minority talking about my moral stability or something else and I'll never get the job." Robert added, "Having AIDS has made me want to reduce the garbage in my life. If people knew, I wonder if the students would freak out—boycott my class. We've all heard stories about the discrimination people with AIDS face. I don't need that."

The apprehension about job discrimination was evident from each individual. These fears in general revolved around promotion and tenure. Don admitted that most junior faculty had concerns about tenure and promotion, but for gay faculty an added burden existed:

I can't separate my feelings of insecurity from my feelings of being a gay man. I think most junior professors have a tough time; your sexual orientation only amplifies it. I see my colleagues making decisions about hiring and I see how irrational most decisions are. Somebody last week said we shouldn't hire someone because she didn't "feel good" about the person—and that was it! These same kind of comments get made for promotion and tenure; that's where being too gay, too public, comes in.

The perceptions of these gay professors revolve around the need to lead their public lives as faculty in a hidden manner. Some individuals feel that part of being a "public teacher"—a role model—is compromised by their private lives; others believe that their private lives will jeopardize their employment if the information becomes public. Indeed, Don went so far as to say that his choices of area of research and department in part had depended on his sexual orientation: "I have felt safer in data-based research than in qualitative or ethnographic research," he explained, "because I don't have to reveal myself." Don also had a choice of entering a College of Education or a College of Social Science. "The reason I chose a social science department instead of something like a College of Education is that I thought social science would be less homophobic than a College of Education. That was a conscious choice. I thought about it."

An individual's fear about job security vis-à-vis tenure is logical, but such a fear does not adequately take into consideration those faculty like Bruce who have tenure; in fact, Bruce is a full professor who has garnered a significant amount of prestige and prominence as a scholar in his field. He also has received many awards at Normal State. As Bruce pointed out, "It's not just tenure you have to worry about":

You need promotion to full professor and other titles you might gain. The problem is not so much in your department where probably everyone knows you. It's the anonymous committees that make decisions about who gets what award. It's easier to use your prejudices if you don't know the person.

What individuals know about one another returns us to the point made in the earlier section about how bisexual, lesbian, and gay people live hidden lives. Don pointed out, "I remember going to a conference and everybody brought out pictures of their kids. It's difficult to show I have an identity—that I'm not this sexless unmentionable doing things in the dark." Robert added, "I wouldn't think of putting a picture up in my office of my partner." Jack continued, "When a male student comes to my office I always make sure there's something between us like a desk. The door is always open. I say to myself this is stupid, this is paranoid, but I also know that it's not stupid." Bruce summed up, "At my previous university I might have brought a partner to a party, but I wouldn't do it here. That would be unacceptable."

The comments highlight the conscious choices faculty make to hide their lives about the most mundane activities. One individual fears putting a picture up in an office; another shies away from office parties; and a third erects artificial barriers in his office. Each of these acts offers at least two interpretations. First, individuals are cognizant about the trouble their private lives will cause in a public arena. Second, the solutions that are proffered with regard to how to overcome the problems are coping strategies designed to aid the individual in realigning his identity to the demands of the power of the norm rather than in restructuring the norm.

Bruce offered one coping strategy, "When I first arrived and realized the situation, how conservative it was, well I just traveled to other cities, to get away." Robert suggested another way to cope, "This place is like others. I've always had two lives. My work life where I know the rules, and then my gay life. When I want to be gay, I have gone to the cities and the bars." Don added, "I've learned that it's okay to say I'm gay if it's not too obvious, if I'm genderless. So when I get tenure, I can take a few more chances, just a few. There will always be consequences." Jack's ideas about how to deal with problems were in transition:

Here's a contradiction, a hypocrisy on my part. I tell students to be vocal, not to accept being pushed around, but I won't always speak up.

My views are changing. Thank God Rosa Parks didn't sit down in the back of the bus. I used to be appalled by ACT-UP but now I understand that social change often won't happen because it's supposed to, but people have to be pushed.

The manner in which these men cope, then, is primarily through masking their identities as gay men. Even if they do not hide their sexual orientation, the act of revealing, of "coming out," provides additional strain for individuals such as Don. In addition to their own internal fortitude, the support network on which they rely is primarily other gay men. "I hang around the bar, go to the potlucks," said Don. Robert also acknowledged Normal State's support network, "There is a supportive environment here—faculty, staff, students, the AIDS support group. It helps you deal with it, that you're not the only one." Bruce, too, enjoyed the social side of the gay community: "When I don't travel, I enjoy the potlucks. It's very relaxed, private. You can meet people."

One might wonder if the comments of these four individuals are idiosyncratic. Is Don justified in saying that merely walking into a gay bar and being seen by his department chair could possibly provoke a negative comment and perhaps have adverse consequences on his career? Is Robert's concern about the possibility of his facing discrimination because he has AIDS warranted or merely a fear on his part? Indeed, Jack pointed out that sometimes he feels his worries about disclosure are "stupid and paranoid." Such questions relate to my comment at the start of the chapter about the generalizability of four individuals' stories.

If one accepts the results of two surveys of a random sample of faculty and students at Normal State, then we might reasonably conclude that the concerns of Don, Robert, Bruce, and Jack are legitimate (LaSalle & Rhoads, 1992). For example, 50 percent of the Normal State student body are afraid to go to certain areas because they do not want to be labeled "one of them," and 65 percent are afraid of having a gay, lesbian, or bisexual roommate or professor. About half of the student sample said they would tell a derogatory gay, lesbian, or bisexual joke. Thus, a significant number of Normal State's community hold negative attitudes about gays. Further, an even larger number do not have any explicit contact with gay people. Eighty-seven percent of the respondents to the faculty and staff survey, for example, said they had no friends who were lesbian or gay.

Studies of other campuses reveal similar findings. A recent article (Tierney, 1992a) reports on a study done by the University of Oregon that states that "the university environment is neither consistently safe for, nor tolerant of, nor academically inclusive of, lesbians, gay men, and bisexuals." A UCLA study found that lesbian, gay, and bisexual students are "significantly more likely than their heterosexual counterparts to have experienced problems associated with harassment, discrimination, and loneliness." Forty-five percent of the lesbian, gay, and bisexual respondents at the University of Massachusetts–Amherst had experienced verbal abuse. Seventy-six percent of all gay, lesbian, and bisexual respondents to a Rutgers survey knew individuals who had been victimized. Fifty-seven percent of the respondents to a similar survey at Yale reported fears for their safety. Indeed, a consistent finding in virtually every campus report done on this topic is that a climate of oppression and invisibility exists on campus. It is at this point that it is important to return to our discussion of the ideology and culture of an institution and how heterosexism and homophobia operate to reinforce the power of the norm.

STRUCTURING INVISIBILITY, UNVEILING MASKS

The Ideology of the Closet

Eve Sedgwick (1990) has pointed out how contemporary sexual identities are consistently blurred so that everyone, especially those in the minority, are in a perpetual state of anxiety. Following Foucault, Sedgwick believes that the power of the norm achieves its goal—conformity—by constantly manipulating these identities so that one is forever kept off balance and out of control. At Normal State, those individuals who think of themselves as gay are indeed "kept off balance" and not in control of giving voice to their sexual identity. Instead, they feel the need to mask who they are and to accede to the power of the norm.

Foucault notes, "There is no binary division to be made between what one says and what one does not say; we must try to determine the different ways of not saying such things. . . . There is not one but many silences, and they are an integral part of the strategies that underlie and permeate discourses" (1980b, p. 27). What Foucault means is illustrated by the comments of Robert, Jack, Bruce, and Don. The manner in which they define and interpret their gay identities is not uniform. Their silence exists in a variety of discursive notions about how their public roles get circumscribed by their private lives as gay men. Conversely, their private lives are also encircled by the public persona of the faculty member. Bruce's public role as a full professor reflects on how he wants to articulate his private life. His unwillingness to enter the gay bar, Friendly's, where his private life would be made "public" exists in relation to his public role as a professor. "I don't want to meet my students in front of the bar," he said. "I don't want to establish that kind of relationship."

Don has discovered that it is "okay to be gay," but the indefiniteness of his position as an assistant professor forces him "not to be too gay." As a double minority, or perhaps triple since he has AIDS, Robert finds himself in conflict not only with the tentative professorial role of an untenured faculty member who is gay, but also with his roles as a well-respected [minority] rights advocate, and as an individual coping with AIDS. Indeed, Robert's public role gets defined in large part by way of his race, and his private life by way of his sexual orientation. He thinks of himself as a person of color and acts publicly in that manner by conducting research, testifying at Congressional hearings, and sponsoring cultural activities that relate to his race. Yet his private life as a gay man with AIDS now unalterably impacts with whom he associates and the way he is able to conduct that public life.

As Sedgwick notes, "Closetedness is a performance initiated as such by the speech act of a silence—not a particular silence, but a silence that accrues particularity by fits and starts, in relation to the discourse that surrounds and differentially constitutes it" (1990, p. 3). The discourses that "surround" Normal State act in concert with the ideological formulations of the institution. These formulations act to marginalize people by the dualism inherent in their private and public lives. Because we assume that everyone is similar, differences act to disturb the norm, which, in turn, reinforces a culture of silence for those who are different. As we have seen, this silence acts in a variety of ways. Individuals hide certain aspects of their lives or they absent themselves from public ceremonies. This impulse to hide, the ideology of silencing, is what Sedgwick has called "the epistemology of the closet [which] has given an overarching consistency to gay culture and identity throughout this century" (1990, p. 68). As with any other totalizing epistemology—one that has silenced women or made African Americans invisible, for example—the question turns to how to develop possibilities for change and liberation.

To reiterate, educational institutions have ideologies that are enacted by way of an organization's culture. These ideologies reflect the social and historical contexts in which the institutions reside. Specifically, an ideology of silencing structures the way lesbian and gay people live at institutions such as Normal State. On the one hand, we see institutional policies pertaining to universalized statements of nondiscrimination that do not mention the word "gay," and, on the other hand we find policies privileging heterosexuals, for example, through health and educational benefits given only to married couples. The heterosexist logic is that no one should be discriminated against; however, at the same time, norms are maintained that make those who are different invisible. Implicitly and explicitly we have an ideology that asserts that everyone is—or should be—the same, for if everyone is the same, then difference is inconsequential.

LIGHTING THE CLOSET: RECONFIGURING DIFFERENCE AND IDENTITY

The quotation from Pirandello at the start of this chapter highlights the way life has been for Robert, Don, Bruce, Jack, and countless other gay faculty. Yet as with the four gay faculty discussed here, an individual who has been silenced often "knows how to wear his mask." The time has come, however, for this particular mask—that which hides and obscures one's gay identity—to become unnecessary and to be put away. By saying that, however, I offer two cautions that pertain to the cultural politics of visibility. One concern has to do with the purpose of gay visibility; the second has to do with how we define difference and identity.

The Meaning of Visibility

To be sure, people who are extreme homophobes also would like to "unmask" gay people, especially gay teachers, so that they will not be able to teach. Obviously, the fears of Robert, Bruce, Don, and Jack derive in part from their belief not simply that they will be unmasked, but that such an unveiling will have harmful consequences. Such an assumption has historical and contextual truth in the sense that people who have been unveiled have often been harmed. My argument here, however, is not that someone's sexual orientation should be simplemindedly exposed for all the world to see; it is rather that we must illuminate the ideological structures within which the cultural politics of everyday life are conducted. The goal is to come to terms with why we have created a system that privileges some and makes others invisible.

What are the relations of power that structure inequity for gays and lesbians in academe? Such a question reorients analyses away from deciding whether to include lesbians and gays as yet another group in a multicultural setting, and toward an understanding of the modes of domination that must be challenged and destroyed if we are to build a truly democratic workplace. The point is that unless we reconceptualize our models of community, we will maintain an allegiance to an ideological system that constantly defines and separates according to a norm based on implicit relations of power.

Defining Difference/Defining Identity

I need to be particularly clear about the purpose of "lighting closets." I am not suggesting that gay men and lesbians should come out of the academic closet so that we become like everyone else. Indeed, our difference is a strength that we ought to capitalize on in a fashion similar to the way people of color also may use their race and ethnicity as a strength. "Understanding marginality as position and place of resistance," notes bell hooks, "is crucial for oppressed, exploited, colonized people. . . . These margins have been sites of repression and sites of resistance" (1990, p. 151). The point here is that our unique identity has been socially constructed in a manner that has been defined in any number of ways—as aberrant, deviant, a shortcoming, or a weakness. We must recognize such definitions for what they are—social constructions that privilege heterosexuality and sanction homophobia—and engage in the process of redefinitions. Examples such as the Black Pride movement, Black History month, or Gay Pride week underscore how different groups have tried to reconstruct for themselves and for society what it means to be different.

Yet in a postmodern world that subscribes to critical theory, we need to reconstruct not simply how we think about a particular group, but also the categories we have used to define individuals and groups. In doing so, we decenter norms and populate the border zones of society. As Jonathan Rutherford notes:

We can use the word difference as a motif for that uprooting of certainty. . . . As an approach to cultural politics it can help us make sense of what is happening: it can be a jumping off point for assembling new practices and languages, pulling together a diversity of theories, politics, cultural experiences and identities into new alliances and movements. Such a politics wouldn't need to subsume identities into an underlying totality that assumes their ultimately homogeneous nature (1990, p. 10).

I am suggesting that the unveiling of masks and the "lighting of closets" is primarily a critique of essentialism and monoculturalism, which is why I have used the term *cultural politics*. How we define identity is not simply a neutral act divorced from power and politics. Such an assumption is fundamentally different from the modernist concept of multiculturalism. However genuine that liberal modernism may have been in its concern for democratic pluralism, it failed because it did not fully come to terms with how power operates in institutions and society. The liberal idea to help people speak, but not to attack the structures and categories that create disablement, falls far short of what I am suggesting.

The critical postmodernist assumes that the act of redefinition, of necessity, brings into question norms and values that have anchored society and formed the basis for oppression. Thus, when we struggle to come to terms with identity, we acknowledge that we will arrive not with a consensual and unitary definition of identity, but instead with multiple and conflicting definitions. "Behind the quest for identity," notes Jeffrey Weeks, "are different and often conflicting values" (1990, p. 89). Identity defines the individual in one way and not another—identity is difference, and in an organization based on agape, the participants need to come to terms with how to recognize and to honor difference.

We must break apart the notion that identity is fixed, as if time and context have nothing to do with our definitions; instead, we seek to uncover how the individual is constantly redescribed by institutional and ideological mechanisms of power. The Foucauldian assumption here is that the force of society is not toward human freedom, but instead that power and ideology seek to constrain and return us to the norm.

As noted, if we see identity as constantly redescribed and constructed, then we also interpret an individual as inhabiting potentially multiple identities that may be confusing and contradictory. Robert was perhaps the clearest example of an individual who had to deal with issues of race, gender, sexual orientation, and class as he struggled with AIDS. Again, we ought not see these multiple identities as inherently problematic, but as definitional sites that help us come to terms with the values we share with others.

By outlining our differences we also find commonalities. "As part of education for critical consciousness in black communities," notes hooks, "it must be continually stressed that our struggle against racism, our struggle to recover from oppression and exploitation, are inextricably linked to all struggles to resist domination" (1989, p. 125). The point is not to assume that all oppression is synonymous, which it clearly is not, but rather to struggle to comprehend how different oppressive forces are linked. How are the conditions that circumscribe racism similar and different from those that define homophobia? How do class and gender oppression differ? Finally, we answer these questions—we define identity—neither in a determined manner nor through an abstract academic understanding of the Other; we come to terms with ourselves and others through mutual engagement founded on praxis and agape.

CONCLUSION

Adrienne Rich has noted:

It takes some strength of soul—and not just individual strength, but collective understanding—to resist this void, this nonbeing, into which you are thrust, and to stand up, demanding to be seen and heard. To make yourself visible, to claim that your experience is just as real and normative as any other . . . can mean making yourself vulnerable. But at least you are not doing the oppressor's work, building your own closet (1986, p. 199).

In a community based on agape and hope, conflict is inevitable if the multiple voices of different groups are to be heard. The lack of conflict either means that particular groups have been silenced and made invisible or that a democratic workplace based on the acceptance of difference has not been reached. The aim here has been to interrogate the ideology and culture of one postsecondary institution in order to unveil how a particular group has been silenced and forced into public conformity; individuals must simultaneously fit within the norm while at the same time they are made to feel abnormal.

In conclusion, I return to the initial comments in this chapter. The documenting of people's lives is important because when we do so, we are engaged in an act of construction of our present worlds. To be sure, the detailing of the life of anyone who has been invisible, such as Don, Robert, Jack, or Bruce, is important simply for its narrative; the recovering of history and the developing of voice are central to the project of critical postmodernism. Yet I have not been arguing that critical postmodernists simply develop a "catalogue of silenced lives" as if the act of recording absolves us of further activity. Instead, I am suggesting that developing voice is a form of historical documentation that tells us how we live now so that we may change. As Stuart Hall notes, "Cultural identity is a matter of becoming as well as being. It belongs to the future as much as to the past. Cultural identities come from somewhere, have histories. But like everything which is historical, they undergo constant transformation"

(1990, p. 225). Thus, the telling of four people's lives gives us ideas about the nature of academe—its ideological definitions and how it gets played out on the terrain of culture.

How we come to terms with these voices—whether we silence them or ignore them, or try to understand how we fit into these public/private dichotomies—gives us a sense of how we are to act in postsecondary institutions, and what the purpose of education ought to be. If we believe that gay voices should be silenced as aberrant, then one vision of the university will be enacted. If we believe that gay voices are simply others to add to a multicultural chorus, then another vision based on as-similationist norms will be envisioned. And if we believe that gay voices are to be encouraged in order to help all of us understand the different ways we are positioned subjects in society, then yet another organizational possibility occurs. This last vision is the hope of this text, and we now turn to a discussion of structure and decision making in academe, in order to investigate how the ideas of these first three chapters are played out through a complex set of organizational strategies.

Chapter Four

Culture and Alienation: Discovering Voice, Discovering Identity

Throughout the last decade, perhaps the most discussed topic in higher education has pertained to the measurement of student outcomes. In one form or another, researchers have undertaken studies about how one might measure a particular institution's learning environment. The discussion has proceeded from three perspectives: (1) effectiveness, (2) quality, and (3) assessment. Most recently, proponents of Total Quality Management (TQM) have sought to combine these three topics into one overarching schema (Marchese, 1991; Ewell, 1991). Researchers and policy analysts have asked the following: What is an effective institution? How do we measure quality? What indicators may we use to assess a college?

Finite resources and increased costs presumably have forced institutions to concern themselves with these topics. Although each topic—effectiveness, quality, and assessment—has investigated postsecondary institutions from different angles, as shown through discussions surrounding TQM, the three perspectives share many common assumptions and concerns. Students are now viewed as consumers, and institutions are markets that compete for consumer preferences. The external environment, whether seen as hostile or friendly, demands increased attention. Individuals and organizations from outside the institution, whether they be a secretary of education, an accrediting agency, a foundation officer, a business, or a state legislator, have become key participants in shaping the discourse of American higher education. Goals that are tied to demonstrable outcomes also have taken on increased importance.

The purpose of this chapter is to bring into question the manner in which this study has proceeded. As I noted in Chapter 1, although no one disputes that colleges and universities must pay attention to how they manage their resources, I suggest that discussions about assessment and student outcomes have done little to enhance teaching and learning in postsecondary institutions. In contrast to Deep Springs College's internal concerns for assessment, calls for assessing the quality of higher education in general have forced institutional participants to concentrate on externally mandated goals that have lessened a concern for the processes with which individuals interact with one another.

To highlight the argument, I offer a case study of Sherman College (a pseudonym), a private liberal arts institution. We will hear the participants of Sherman reflect on their college and what issues they believe are important. Sherman is a useful example because we gain a portrait of an institution that is not yet in the throes of institutional assessment, although some individuals would like to move in that direction. As we shall see, little agreement exists about the specific goals of the institution, or the manner in which teaching and learning should occur. Thus, we move on in this chapter from a discussion of individual identity (the focus of the previous chapter) to one of collective identity. In so doing, I discuss the parameters of organizational culture and consider what mechanisms we might use to create a community based on difference rather than similarity. Paradoxically, then, I consider how a collective identity that embraces difference instead of uniformity might be shaped and formed. By *organizational culture*, I mean those symbolic and ideological aspects of the institution that help frame identity. By *collective identity*, I mean those equifinal processes that members employ to help determine organizational processes, goals, and meanings. In the discussion that follows the case study, I pose two related questions:

1.   How might the culture of Sherman College become more focused toward a collective identity; and

2.   What would assessment look like from a critical postmodern perspective?

My purpose, then, is to offer an alternative opinion to the prevailing notion that postsecondary institutions ought to become more forcefully concerned with measuring and assessing student outcomes as determined by external forces. To be sure, colleges and universities must acknowledge the contexts in which they reside and they ought to have a clearer sense than they do at present about student outcomes. Yet my goal here is to

suggest that an overreliance on measuring and delineating student outcomes inevitably (1) reduces a concern for understanding the processes
taken to achieve those goals; (2) increases institutional norms that
privilege some and silence others; and (3) lessens the bonds of community
and organizational agape.

SHERMAN COLLEGE: CULTURE AND VOICE

Sherman College is more than one hundred years old and has an
enrollment that hovers around two thousand students. There are about 150
faculty, the vast majority of whom hold Ph.D.'s. Sherman has steadily
raised its tuition, especially over the last decade, which has resulted in two
significant changes. First, for the most part, first-generation college-goers
or individuals associated with the church that started the institution are no
longer an important part of the student body. Second, the market from
which the admissions office draws its students has grown much smaller.
"We're dealing with an increasingly affluent clientele," explained the
admissions director. "I hope it's leveled off, but in the eighties we said that
10 percent of high school classes could come here, and now it's more like
5 percent."

The college's response to its changing student body has been both
indifferent and dramatic. "We still get the same kind of students," related
one longtime faculty member. The individual's colleague agreed, "We get
average students. We got them when I came here in the sixties, and we get
them today." "The social life has always been strong here," added a third
individual. "We're always working on having students become more
concerned about the academic side of things." A fourth person continued,
"We still sell the college the same way we did ten years ago—individual
attention, small classes, a community atmosphere. That kind of thing." So
in one aspect, although the student body has become more affluent and
admissions must draw from a smaller pool, the life of the college has not
changed.

However other individuals pointed to changes this new clientele had
required. "We've got yuppies coming here, and we cater to their needs.
Look at the campus," commented one individual. The individual referred
to the significant face-lift the campus had received during the last decade.
Virtually every building had been renovated, and there were also new
additions such as a library and a student center. "Students expect more,
and we try to give it to them," explained another person.

In addition, the increased tuition has meant that the admissions office at times has been unable to attract students for a particular department or to attract students of color. An admissions officer elaborated:

We are tuition driven. I must have a certain number of students show up on campus. I can't come in 150 short. You've got to produce what drives your budget. That means I have to concentrate in particular areas. Sometimes a department chair will come to me and say he wants more students or better students, and I understand what he means. But if I spend my time in chasing after one or two students for a particular department I will not meet my goal, the college's goal. That means diversity is a problem too. I don't know how we get these people to come here. There are just not enough of them in the pool. It's tremendously draining.

As the student clientele has changed, so have the faculty. "We have a more professional faculty now," pointed out one faculty member. "The older faculty are more a part of the community; they have more of a sense of the college-as-family," added another professor. "Younger faculty see their job differently, the balance between teaching and research [has changed]," said a third faculty member.

Another person explained that the most significant change he had seen at Sherman took place in the early eighties when a new president and academic dean changed the promotion and tenure process: "All of a sudden, faculty were told they were supposed to do something that they hadn't thought was part of their job—research and publication." New faculty seem to accept the new requirements, but the changes have been met with resistance on the part of some individuals. "The result has not changed anything for the younger ones, the ones who come up for promotion from assistant to associate," said one individual. "The problem is that for a lot of individuals who were here when the process changed, they've been stuck as associate professors. It's left a degree of ill will."

The "ill will" that the individual referred to was not only an effect of the change in promotion-and-tenure policy, but also of the manner in which it was done. When a new president arrived over a decade ago, he decided that an academic dean needed to be hired from the outside; up to that time, the provost had always come from, and returned to, the faculty. "Much more management came with that president," said one faculty member. A second professor pointed out, "I know people will disagree, but both the previous president and provost did exactly what they needed to do. The president brought in money, and the provost bit the bullet on some difficult issues like tenure. We became more professional." The professor was right, however, about those who disagreed: "The previous academic dean was a disaster," said one individual. "He was exactly what we did not need," said another. A third commented, "Faculty morale sank when this person came and rose when he left."

At present a new president and new provost have arrived, and they have engendered a degree of goodwill, although the suspicion remains "about what they are up to in Sherman Hall" (the administration building). As two students laughed, "No matter what happens, someone will say, 'Administration did it,' " said one. The second student added, "It's like decisions happen, and then they ask for your input. It's lame." The faculty in large part concurred with the second student's perception. When the new president arrived, he had a series of small group meetings during which he listened to all of the faculty's complaints, ideas, and suggestions. As the president himself related:

I wanted to get to know faculty quickly. We talked about the college. I wanted to get a sense of the college. The cynicism faculty felt was real. Out of those conversations people started talking about projects. I then synthesized what they said and set up a group of task forces. It was a process of strategic planning. It really was their ideas. I didn't come in here with a hidden agenda, but I know in some corners suspicions remain.

The faculty welcomed these meetings, but they were not so willing to accept that the president did not have an agenda. "We had these cozy afternoon teas," said one, "but you always felt he had ideas up his sleeve that he wanted to get us to bring up." Another person added, "After these talks, he set up the task forces, and we were to decide particular issues. One issue was about student life in the freshman year. In the middle of it all, the president announced he totally reorganized student affairs, which made our work worthless." Nevertheless, the president and his provost still had support and a high degree of goodwill among the various constituencies on campus. Both individuals were seen as active, energetic administrators who, in general, had the best interests of the college in mind with their efforts.

Within eighteen months after the president had arrived, he and the provost had begun a number of initiatives that had borne fruit. The two of them wrote a grant to a major foundation for 1.5 million dollars to stimulate the teaching and learning environment. The president received money from another foundation to endow chairs. The federal government provided additional funds for academic programs. The administration started an ambitious capital campaign that gave every indication of succeeding. "He had a helluva year with the foundations," summed up one individual. "This was the proverbial 'hit the ground running,' " added another.

Two related points about these actions highlight the culture and voice of Sherman College; *culture* pertains to the symbolic life of the institution, and *voice* refers to who is actively involved in the decisions of the college. First, none of these proposals needed faculty approval, and second, the manner in which these ideas were developed and communicated to the faculty underscores a community alienated from itself. My point here is that one might anticipate that such creative ideas will stimulate a sense of camaraderie and institutional excitement. However, although I did not hear antipathy among the various groups at Sherman, neither did I find a sense of institutional excitement. That is, the administration had developed a rather ambitious agenda, but as we will see, the initial successes that occurred did not seem to provide a more cohesive sense of community or greater involvement on the part of the college's constituencies; rather, in general, it resulted in feelings of estrangement or parochialism.

In part, the lack of community derives from a decision-making process that fosters fragmentation. "If you feel you have a good idea you have to sell it to someone," one individual commented. An administrator said, "People often feel they have a good idea, but it gets squashed by the faculty." A second administrator explained:

We used to operate on the assumption that everyone had to be on board. But we'd get nothing done. We'd bring it to the faculty, and it would die. In a way we try to circumvent the process now. We do things that don't need faculty approval. We think, "Gee, isn't there a way to do this, to get it moving without taking it to the faculty?" It's not authoritarian. The president gets an idea, brings it informally to different groups of the faculty, brings in those who are the most likely opponents, and gradually transfers ownership to the faculty. But we don't begin with taking it to them.

Faculty members generally agreed with this analysis. "We seem to have consciously given away power, power over student life, for example," said one person. "We don't have faculty leaders, really. We have leaders on specific issues," said another. A third person said, "It's like the joke where the guy says, 'My wife makes all the unimportant decisions—where we live, what we eat, which neighbors we see. I make the important decisions, like what our relationship should be with China.' The faculty think we have power because we decide things about the curriculum, but we don't, not really."

Both faculty and administrators at Sherman believe that the faculty have power and control over the academic side of the institution. Many individuals cite an example of a few years ago when the development office tried to raise money for faculty positions in "leadership and management." "The money was there," sighed the development officer. "We could have raised substantial sums of money, but the faculty felt they were not consulted, and it blew up in our faces." Essentially, Sherman's liberal arts faculty felt that the administration was trying to make the college more "professional," and they rejected the idea. "Looking back," said one person, "it wasn't handled correctly. No one was going behind the faculty's backs, but they weren't consulted, and they just said no." Their rejection of the idea was evidence to many people that the faculty held power at Sherman. However, there were few other examples that individuals were able to point to as projects that the faculty either initiated or stopped. "We go about our business—small things, daily things, that's life here."

This perceived lack of power on the part of the faculty leads to my second point about the manner in which the initiatives developed by the president and provost were communicated to the faculty. When asked their opinions concerning the 1.5 million dollar grant—a substantial sum for a small institution—no one knew anything about the grant. "Is that the one about summer funding?" queried one individual. Asked another, "Are you talking about the faculty positions?" A third said, "I think I might have heard about it, but it was many months ago." The public relations officer commented:

I found out about it when we applied; people in administration were excited. But I never read the proposal. When we got it, the provost told the faculty, and I wrote up a press release according to what he said. It was very unassuming. I sent it along to the foundation and they came back to me and said, "We think this grant is exciting, it's big, and you don't portray that." Well, I hadn't because that's the way the provost told the faculty, real low-key. We're always afraid of the faculty thinking we've done things behind their backs.

Thus, even though several significant activities have been taking place, the administration consciously downplayed their importance, in part, to lessen the possibility that the faculty would be angered that they were not consulted prior to a particular proposal's submission. Rather than portray a new project as something that has happened, the administration attempted to point toward a direction with the hope that the faculty desired to move there.

Further, Sherman's culture is one that eschews highly innovative projects; to communicate to the faculty that a dramatic new initiative had begun would be to violate one of the norms of the institution. "This is not a bold place," said an individual with a long history at Sherman. "We have protected ourselves from getting into fads, but we also have never been a leader." "We always ask if it's been done before," commented another person. "We applaud ourselves for creating something like Women's Studies, but we did it ten years after everyone else," said a third individual. "The faculty finally agreed to student evaluation of classes," continued a fourth person, "and we thought it was a big deal." Explained one person, "If this makes sense: for a conservative institution, we are liberal."

The point is that on campus resides a particular ethos that many see as parochial and/or demoralizing. Yet this sense of alienation is odd; people are not angry with one another, and they do not openly discuss their unhappiness or desire to leave. "People will say, 'How are things going in your department' and you'll say, 'Pretty well,' but the sense exists that we're missing something in general," commented one faculty member. A second added, "I suppose faculty always say they are demoralized, but this is of a particular kind. I enjoy teaching. I enjoy my department. I enjoy my colleagues, most of them. But something is missing here." A third person disagreed slightly, "I'm not demoralized. Morale isn't a problem. It's just that the acceptable attitude here is to be cynical and skeptical. People are manipulated and feel it." A fourth person concluded, "I want to know what the attitude problem is."

Although individuals may have "an attitude problem," they also tend to believe that the institution offers a quality education. "Students get a very good education at Sherman," responded one faculty member. "The teaching of our faculty is excellent," said another. "The quality of the faculty can't be questioned, that's certain," commented another. "It's a quality curriculum, yes. Many students go on to graduate school," added another professor.

Sherman assesses quality in an indirect fashion, such as if students continue on to graduate school. "You know who are the good faculty because students talk about them," said one individual. "In some departments, faculty sit in on one another's classes on occasion. We all evaluate the classes of the younger ones, up for promotion and tenure," said another. The institutional research officer pointed to the retention rate, "Seventy-eight percent graduate within five years." Two faculty members mentioned that they talk about teaching with other faculty in the freshman-year symposium. Said one, "You get an idea about how someone teaches when you hear him talk about a particular reading." The provost added, "I'm a seat-of-the pants administrator. I'll view success of an idea in terms of how much ownership is out there, how much excitement has been generated, and if we have money to continue it, of course."

When individuals were pressed further about assessment and how they knew their institution was "excellent," they again exhibited a sense of low self-esteem or of feeling demoralized. "We lack a common vision, and we need someone to articulate that shared vision whom we trust," commented one person. "We disagree on what students should learn, so how could we ever have a common assessment instrument?" asked another. A third person said, "Assessment is not an issue here; it's never brought up." A fourth person commented, "There is a lack of articulation of what the goals of the college are." A fifth person responded, "This is not a community. I feel disenfranchised in faculty meetings. I've been told that younger faculty shouldn't talk in the faculty meeting. We feel threatened and left out." A sixth person concurred, "Sometimes I think we exist in an atmosphere of paranoia, but it's unjustified. I do know that we are not a community, not a group that comes together. We get letters that begin 'Dear Employee.' That about sums it up, doesn't it?" Another individual "summed up" in similar fashion. When asked what kind of institution Sherman should be in five years, the person responded:

I want an institution that's more self-confident. There's a feeling now that we're not as good as we say we are. We need to believe in who we are. We're defensive. I don't think people believe we're working toward the same goal. There's a sense of anxiety here that makes us behave in ways we shouldn't. On an individual level, people are okay. And this is not a place coming apart at the seams. But I want a sense of excitement. Even faculty question if we can pull something off. I wouldn't want to work in anything other than a college, but we need a sense of purpose, of pulling together, of seeing how exciting Sherman can really be.

DISCUSSION

Here, then, is an organization that many will assume is well-situated. The financial outlook is strong. The campus is in good physical shape. A dynamic new administrative team has developed several ideas, many of which already have taken seed and begun to grow. Although Sherman exists in a precarious environment with regard to student clientele and the rising cost of tuition, unlike countless other small liberal arts colleges, the institution is not in any grave danger. Scanning the environment for threats and opportunities is a necessity, but it has not engendered any dramatic shifts in institutional mission or purpose. And, too, no serious internal problems exist on campus. Students are not poised to take over any buildings; no union is set to go on strike; and the faculty are not contemplating a vote of no confidence in their president. Indeed, the faculty and administration have relatively cordial relations. Surely a president or professor at a beleaguered institution where salary freezes, cutbacks, and declines in student enrollment have become the norm, or where different constituencies no longer talk with one another, would view Sherman College with a mixture of jealousy and admiration.

Yet Sherman's participants do not voice a similar amount of pride or awareness of their strengths. The individual above commented about the desire for an institution with more "self-confidence." Someone else wanted to know what was the nature of the "attitude problem." Again, individuals are not unhappy in the sense that Sherman has experienced massive departures of faculty or staff. Faculty also say that they think students receive a good education, although they are unsure in a specific sense why they say that.

Sherman is an organization that highlights the implicit nature of culture. The individuals within a culture reach definitions of what they mean by excellence and quality not simply by externally mandated standards, but by ongoing definitions of their own self-worth. These definitions are enacted through any number of symbolic artifacts such as ceremonies and rituals, but they also occur through daily interactions (Tierney, 1988a; Tierney, 1988b). And out of the language and symbols of our daily lives, we define our relationships to one another and the patterns of our actions within the organization. Individuals certainly bring preconceived notions about what they expect from an organization, and the organization has a structure and history prior to an individual's entry that defines what is expected; but culture is malleable. It is constructed and interpreted. All individuals are able to shape the organization's culture, and to be shaped by it. To be sure, some individuals such as a president or provost have specific influence due to their positions, but my assumption is that no one is powerless. From a critical postmodern perspective, the struggle is to enable individuals to utilize their voices in defining communal values. Michael Katz has written that the ideal university

should be a community of persons united by collective understandings, by common and communal goals, by bonds of reciprocal obligation, and by a flow of sentiment which makes the preservation of the community an object of desire, not merely a matter of prudence or a command of duty. Community implies a form of social obligation governed by principles different from those operative in the marketplace and the state (1987, p. 179).

Like a high-achieving millionaire who is perceived by many as successful but who actually feels quite alone, Sherman College may be an institution poised for excellence, yet actually alienated from itself. The comments from various individuals at Sherman point out an institution in which a sense of community and social fellowship is absent. Several individuals commented about the parochial nature of the college; individuals enjoyed the company of those in their immediate vicinity such as their department, but they did not have a sense of a community at Sherman. One may ask if an organization needs community and fellowship; the answer returns us to the purpose of this chapter.

In Chapter 1, I commented how we often accept commonplace assertions as facts if we either know them to be, or believe them to be, true. North Dakota's cold winters, I noted, do not have to be lived through to be believed. I went one step further, however, and pointed out that if we contextualize certain commentary, we also find agreement. In general, women faculty share a common experience that men do not have and hence cannot interpret in similar fashion. Gay and lesbian students might have common interpretations of dorm life that heterosexual students might not understand. Similarly, the events at Sherman may not resonate to all readers, but in general, American faculty in the late twentieth century probably find a large measure of agreement with the characterization of the lack of community in academe. Over the last few years, a number of works (Boyer, 1990; Bowen & Schuster, 1986; Clark, 1987; Tierney, 1989) have pointed out similar findings from faculty: a lack of collegiality and meaning occur in countless institutions. Individuals in academic institutions seem to desire a sense of affiliation, and they feel that it is missing.

In part, the breakdown of community is not necessarily bad if the definition of community we employ is a romantic notion of "the good old days." For those days were times when women and people of color, among others, were absent from the community. Those days were also times when we held to singular notions of identity so that the academy was primarily populated by one group of people. As I noted, it is not surprising that organizational theorists in academe developed what is commonly called the "collegial model," for it is based on the notion that consensus can be reached because all individuals ultimately subscribe to the same values.

The kind of community that Michael Katz talks about, however, is not based on similarity; rather, it focuses yet again on agape. We are united in a community and culture through mutual desire to understand one another's differences, and from those differences to forge alliances that, in effect, create a new organizational culture. In suggesting that we create a new organizational culture through the development of a community of difference, I offer two related ideas. First, we must see how this culture differs from a collegial model of community based on norms and similarities. Second, we should reject the liberal notion that suggests that simply by having different people—that is, women and people of color—present on our faculty, we have transformed the culture. As Chandra Mohanty notes:

Creating such cultures is fundamentally about making the axes of power transparent in the context of academic, disciplinary, and institutional structures as well as interpersonal relationships in the academy. . . . Culture itself is thus redefined as incorporating individual and collective memories, dreams, and history that are contested and transformed through the political praxis of day-to-day living (1990, p. 207).

I am suggesting that the struggle at Sherman College is, in many ways, in contradistinction with that at Deep Springs, and, in large part, if the works of Boyer and the other authors mentioned are to be believed, what takes place at Sherman is currently being enacted on numerous other campuses throughout the United States. By claiming that community has been lost, we ought not to look back nostalgically to rediscover a past that was far from perfect, but instead look to how our differences might create communal bonds of fellowship among one another. We create community, then, not through the received wisdom of the ages, but through the present interactions of our hopes for the future. If we do so, we realize that the job of creating communities of difference is not reducible to simple acts of policy or curricular change; rather, collective change is fundamental and contested and needs to occur in all areas of the institution on a daily basis.

In arguing for the development of community in academe, I work from the assumption that to improve the teaching and learning environment in our institutions, an organization's participants need to have common definitions of excellence and quality, and that these definitions necessarily derive from dialogue among one another. If this dialogue concentrates, however, on outcomes and effectiveness, we blur the distinction between educational and corporate worlds by assuming that "bottom lines" exist, that students are "products," and that education is a quantifiable outcome. Such assumptions stand in sharp contrast to a portrait of an educational community that exists through "collective understandings" and "common and communal goals." A lack of discussion of moral understanding, of what ties our community together, weakens the very purpose of an educational institution.

In large part, the manner in which these dialogues take place will tell us as much as the ultimate goals do about the nature of our community and how we determine excellence. The proponents of the assessment movement would have us believe we need to have a greater concern for measuring quality and student outcomes. We are told that change needs to occur in our colleges and universities, but the discussions about the dynamics of such change are absent. I am suggesting that an institution such as Sherman College will be ill-served if it concentrates on measuring effectiveness; instead it ought to spend greater time developing common definitions of what it means by community. The point, of course, is not simply to develop abstract definitions, but rather to engage in discussions about institutional meanings that are in some way related to how we interact with one another. And these meanings are neither static nor rigid; they are fluid, ongoing definitions that get worked out through the communicative processes the members employ in creating a community based on difference.

Discussions about outcomes are inevitably goal-oriented; we want to know what students must achieve. Discussions about community are process-oriented; we want to know what kind of community we desire to build, and we consider how we will do it. Assessment is externally oriented; we develop criteria that enable others to judge us in relation to other institutions. Communal discussions are internally oriented; we engage in dialogue to come to terms with how we are to govern and live with one another. Assessment is a discussion among professionals—in general, administrators—about another group—students. Critical postmodern discussions of community involve all of the community—students, faculty, administrators, and staff. Assessment is a summative dialogue; communal discourse is formative.

The current assessment movement also highlights what counts for knowledge. That is, rather than dispositional knowledge that pertains to the kinds of self-reflexive knowledge that one needs to participate in a democracy, the assessment movement primarily has focused on factual or cognitive knowledge. We test whether students know particular facts or if they are able to conceptualize particular problems accurately. "Dispositional knowledge," write Tierney and Rhoads, "pertains more to the processes one engages in on a daily basis than it does to any fixed endpoint on a multiple choice exam" (forthcoming b, p. 15). I want to stress that my point is obviously neither that factual knowledge is unimportant nor that critical-thinking skills are irrelevant. However, by focusing on assessment and student outcomes rather than on what we want to be as a community and culture, we set the dialogue in one way rather than another. And I am suggesting that dialogues of assessment most often move us away from building communities of difference.

Some will argue that assessment is a way to develop common under-standings about the nature of the organization. Although the possibility exists for discussions about assessment to develop communal bonds of affiliation, there are few examples where this has happened. Assessment sets the parameters of discourse, and such discussions do not turn to the nature of what we are about, but how to achieve a particular goal. Simply stated, communities, like families, do not have goals akin to a business—nor should they. Communities exist through the coming to terms with the parameters of ideas such as social fellowship and obligation. Communities such as Sherman also need to have a sense of unity and purpose; ultimately, such purpose enables individuals to act in concert with one another toward a common vision.

Others will argue that discussions about community inevitably exclude particular individuals and groups and that they do not necessarily create an efficient climate for decision making. However, because discussions about community have the possibility to exclude different groups and individuals, or because they are bureaucratically inefficient, does not mean that we should avoid trying to build academic communities. Discussions of community enable individuals to come to terms with one another in ways that generally do not happen when discourse is framed in terms of meeting demands from the external environment.

Sherman College is a good example of an institution that could provoke conversations either about assessment or community. How might such discussions happen at Sherman College? What would be the advantage of either dialogue?

My concern with a discussion about assessment at Sherman is that often it does not foster a sense of the college and, instead, enables people to stay cloistered in their departments. Rather than bringing people together as an academic community with a common vision of who they are, a discussion of assessment structures the dialogue in terms of objective goals.

In contrast, communal discussions have the potential to enable Sherman's participants to relate to one another so that a common vision might develop. And again, such a vision is created not out of a consensual model but, rather, within a framework where we develop our goals in mutually sustainable conversations of respect that inevitably will give rise to different interpretations of organizational reality. In what follows, I turn to two aspects of communal discourse that underscore the benefits specific to institutions such as Sherman and to academe in general. I raise these topics here to begin a discussion I will concentrate on more fully in Chapter 7. Each point is more strategic in nature than instrumental; developing community is not something that is done by following directions in a "how-to" manual. At the same time, there are strategic options that individuals might consider as they struggle to create community on their own campuses.

The Culture of Community

At present, the structure in which dialogue takes place at Sherman seems to impede the free discussion of ideas rather than enhance them. Indeed, many of the most recent initiatives have been developed in such a way that administrators have been able to circumvent the decision-making process. Faculty in general, and at Sherman in particular, are versed in the art of critique; they are better able to discover the flaws in an idea than they are able to construct a particular program. Yet that is precisely what an organization's participants are now called on to do. What kind of community do they want for one another? The answer to the question in part lies in the way they structure the dialogue.

If the question is brought up in a faculty senate in which students are absent and younger faculty feel as if they must keep quiet, then one kind of answer will be found. If the question is developed in terms of "turf" so that one department feels it has much to lose and another has much to gain, then another kind of answer will be uncovered. And if the president asks the question in order to submit a proposal for the funding of yet another initiative, then still another answer will be reached.

I cannot say that one forum for discussion is better than another, or that there are simple steps to effective decision making about the nature of community. I raise the point about organizational culture, however, because essentially the problems raised here are cultural rather than, for example, fiscal or structural. Sherman is not in fiscal danger. It is not an institution where the president has seized all of the power. And yet the culture of Sherman appears fragmented. On the administrative side, individuals feel that the decision-making process slows them down; on the faculty side, younger professors feel excluded, and older professors feel that they no longer have control over their institutional lives. In all cases, the culture of decision making has worked against the development of community.

The president's conversations with individuals were initially ways to bring everyone into discussions about the nature of community. What did not seem to occur, however, was the development of the community's voice; rather, the president alone was able to implement ideas that he had heard. How might one help develop a culture in which a climate for innovation and change is encouraged? In part, the president and provost had begun a process that ought to be continued: they brought faculty into discussions and encouraged ownership of ideas.

Faculty development is another way to stimulate thinking about how one's own community functions. That is, one way to consider what kind of community we ought to live in is to have a comparative awareness of other communities. The point is to raise individual awareness of different programs, initiatives, and processes in which other institutions engage, rather than simply to be able to gauge how well Sherman is doing in relation to other institutions. To that end, as I will expand on in the next chapter, a faculty's ability to travel to professional meetings or to visit other campuses enables individuals to come to terms with what kind of culture they want. Ultimately, however, the development of voice turns on the manner in which individuals relate to one another.

Activities need to be structured and referenced in terms of how they enhance or detract from coming to terms with institutional identity. From this perspective, countless choices exist in the culture, and decision makers need to be cognizant about which choices enhance institutional identity and which choices obscure or alter an institution's ethos and purpose. Institutional life is in constant change, constant evolution, and those involved in the process have a say in reformulating the culture.

Such an assertion stands in contrast to the belief that institutions are "organized anarchies" (Cohen & March, 1974) in which individuals are replaceable parts, one as good as another. I am working from the assumption that every individual in a community is a valued member with an essential part to play in the development of institutional identity. To foment change, we must encourage diversity toward a specific identity. The contradiction here is that not every individual must move to the same interpretation of reality, but all individuals need to feel a part of the organization. Equifinal processes enable multiple interpretations of the organization in order to achieve unified goals. Such is the purpose of communal decision making.

Assessment from a Critical Postmodern Perspective

I have pointed out two ways assessment has taken place. One framework assesses student abilities: How do students write? How do they do math? The second framework is longitudinal in nature: How much do students know when they arrive at college and how much did they learn by the time they leave? This is a "value-added" approach to assessment. Both frameworks work from standard definitions of knowledge, and quality obviously revolves around high scores. If students score well on a writing exam, or if their scores have dramatically improved while they have been at an institution, then we can say the student has been successful in college.

Obviously, the argument here is not the logical opposite. No one suggests that writing is unimportant. No one hopes that students do not learn a great deal while they are in college. From a critical postmodern perspective, however, we reorient the nature of assessment more in keeping with the self-reflective and communal nature of what takes place at Deep Springs College.

Another specific example of processual assessment that incorporates ideas from this angle is the series of discussions that have taken place at Harvard under the direction of Richard Light (1992). The Harvard Assessment Seminars have engaged students and faculty in ongoing interviews and conversations about the nature of learning and how Harvard's academic life might be improved. The discussions revolve neither around external standards of excellence nor about how much is learned during a student's tenure at Harvard. Instead, the seminars work at improving the culture of teaching and learning by discussing in depth with those involved in the enterprise what they feel about the strengths and weaknesses of Harvard's education. By discussing commonalities and differences, the seminars have eventually developed specific points about how to improve undergraduate education.

Possible objections arise with this example. In many respects, Harvard is as unique as Deep Springs College. Some will argue that Harvard's students are more capable of intellectually oriented discussions than most students. Others will argue that the findings Light and his colleagues developed are inappropriate for the vast majority of institutions. From the ideas advanced here, however, I fundamentally disagree with the first objection and do not feel the second is of concern.

If educational empowerment as I defined it in Chapter 2 is to be employed, then all students are capable and in need of reflective discussions about the nature of their own education. And when such discussions occur, they undoubtedly give rise to specific solutions that are contextually based. Thus, the framework that Harvard has employed is similar to what occurs at Deep Springs and could just as likely happen at Sherman—ongoing discussions about the nature of the institution's education and definitions of knowledge and ultimately, community.

Although the framework from institution to institution may be similar, the definitions will be unique. Obviously, the specific parameters of what Harvard's students need may differ from those of Sherman College and many other institutions. The point is not simply to copy the recommendations of Harvard or any other institution. Instead, what must occur is a commitment to dialogue. A critical theory of assessment is one that reconfigures power and knowledge by way of who is involved, what is discussed, and how we conceptualize the relationship between teacher and student. By engaging in such dialogues, the institution's participants actively work to reform the organization's culture and actively develop community. Students become the architects of their education, and faculty find that what binds them together are not abstract criteria but the processes in which they are involved.

CONCLUSION

Sherman is an intriguing case study of a culture alienated from itself yet still able to function effectively. The president, provost, and others at the college seem to realize this dichotomy and are working to change the life of the institution so it becomes more of a community. Positive steps include the movement toward dialogue with everyon, and the initiatives geared toward creating change where the faculty are active participants. Yet, as noted, because the decision-making structure is perceived as cumbersome, many individuals try to circumvent it, and others feel silenced by it.

I have argued that the road to improvement at Sherman ought not be by way of assessing the quality of academic programs or students in a manner akin to the way we have come to think about assessment. Instead, I have suggested that a focus on the processes of community will enhance the academic enterprise. From this perspective, assessment is not an end product but an ongoing process. Academic quality is not the production of students with particular outcomes, but engages the organization's participants with discussions that enable them to come to terms with their own lives. All individuals are involved in the life and decisions of the community as opposed to a cadre of professionals who direct the organization's outcomes. Teamwork and collaboration are seen as essential, and the empowerment of all individuals, rather than their evaluation, is the goal.

Chapter Five

Critical Leadership and Decision Making in a Postmodern World

Due in large part to the fiscal belt-tightening that occurred throughout the 1980s, administrators have increasingly turned to strategic planning as a decision-making style. The intended goal of strategic planning is to give a cohesive direction and purpose to an institution beset by all too common problems such as declining enrollments, an increasingly competitive marketplace, and a physical plant in dire need of capital improvements.

"Strategic planning," notes one of its central architects, George Keller, "could not have been devised at a better time for American higher education" (1983, p. 118). Keller maintains that, due to the myriad of problems that beset academe, administrators need to have a "battle plan" just as the military have strategies to defeat their enemies. In effect, strategic planning bolsters the rational idea that individuals are not only able to be, but must be, in charge of their own organizational destinies if colleges and universities are to survive.

In this chapter, I offer a case study of an institution that has recently engaged in strategic planning. Huntsville College (a pseudonym) is a small, private liberal arts institution where a president began a strategic plan in a manner that has become commonplace in the world of academe. A new president was hired and one of his first decisions was that the institution needed to have a better sense of where it was going and what it wanted to do. "We didn't know who we were," reflected the president four years after the process had been put in motion. "I thought strategic planning would help us focus more."

My purpose in this chapter is to take issue with assumptions such as the president's and in doing so highlight the underlying tenets of strategic planning and, by inference, leadership. By way of a case study of Huntsville College, I offer a portrait of the different constituencies at Huntsville, their reactions to the manner in which strategic planning was carried out, and their definitions of leadership. The idiosyncrasies we find at Huntsville should not be of concern to us; however, the institution brings into focus larger issues about higher education's purposes and decision-making processes. I suggest that the manner in which administrators manage the institution and the form used for institutional decision making centrally affect how the institution acts and is defined; that is, an analysis of decision making not only tells us what decisions were made by whom, but it also helps explain the culture and ideology of the institution.

Huntsville is also a good case study because the president and the designers of the strategic planning process have tried to create collective decision making based on a collegial model, but as we will see, most individuals are dissatisfied with the outcomes and process. As with so many other institutions, the problems that beset Huntsville do not lend themselves to simpleminded solutions: the replacing of a president or an infusion of funds will not settle all conflicts. In large part, the president and his team have struggled to deal with the college's manifold problems, and they have tried to do so in an equitable manner. Accordingly, I suggest that Huntsville's challenges provide three questions for discussion:

1.   How might we define critical leadership in a postmodern world?
2.   What should be the goal of strategic planning?
3.   What are preliminary organizational points that are based on agape and critical postmodernism?

The chapter is divided into three parts. First, I will offer a brief overview of previous discussions of academic planning and decision making. I will then provide a brief historical sketch of the institution before developing the case study of Huntsville College. In so doing, I discuss the challenges the constituents faced with the strategic planning process. In the third section, I will consider each of the questions raised above.

My point here is not to paint the failure of an institution in its attempts at strategic planning, but rather to highlight the differing perceptions individuals have about the nature of their lives and their institution. My goal is to attempt to reorient academe's definition of leadership and decision making so that it is more in keeping with the discussion raised in the previous chapters. I argue that we ought to move away from developing goals that are externally driven and move toward a concern for internal processes. I suggest that in academe we need to focus our energies more on the internal dynamics with which we coexist with one another and less on perceived external demands from the environment.

STRATEGIC LEADERSHIP AND DECISION MAKING

In the managerial revolution that took place in the 1960s, academic institutions changed from essentially simple organizational forms composed of a handful of administrators and the faculty, to complex organizations in which a variety of individuals took responsibility for numerous managerial tasks. The assumption that a president and academic vice president could simultaneously shoulder responsibilities of a dean of students, development officer, fiscal officer, or a multitude of other organizational roles quickly became an idea of the past. Instead, we observed the proliferation of administrative roles and responsibilities.

To some, the rise of administration and bureaucracy created a cadre of individuals who could also set the direction for the institution. Such a decision-making style, commonly known as *linear strategy*, was in vogue in the 1960s and early 1970s as the idea of administration in academe became increasingly professionalized. "As the word 'linear' suggests," notes Ellen Chaffee, "in this mode, strategy is methodical, direct, sequential, and plan-based" (1989, p. 25). The notion either that an institution existed in the shadow of a college president or that an organization was a collegium where the faculty set the direction fell by the wayside.

Administrative teams composed of president and "cabinet" became the decision makers for colleges and universities. They set goals, generated plans to achieve them, and decided which route was preferable in order to reach their market. Although the president was no longer a charismatic "great man" considered with the likes of Charles Eliot of Harvard or Robert Hutchins of Chicago, a president still maintained sweeping authority over the academic enterprise. Eventually, decision makers felt the need for another decision-making style in large part due to the unpredictability of academe's environment in the 1970s and the multiplicity of goals that colleges and universities had to pursue simultaneously.

The "boom" of the higher education bubble had burst; fewer traditionally-aged students attended academe and less money was available from federal and state governments. Students demanded services, such as day care for their children or health care, that had not been previously needed, and these demands created additional fiscal strains for the institution.

Thus, students of organizational theory rejected the idea that a small group of individuals could set the agenda for an organization irrespective of an external environment, as if the structure were a walled institution that merely needed to define its goals and the rest would follow. Commonly known as *open systems,* these new ideas presaged a vast array of literature about the environment and the need for administrators to take into account the needs of the marketplace.

Linear strategy gave way to *adaptive strategy,* in which individuals in organizations no longer worked in isolation; rather, administrators struggled to adapt to the demands of the external environment. "Students" became "markets." The importance of information that would help decision makers read the market accurately took on increased significance. The assumption was that perfect information was available, and the task of the decision maker was to arrive at the correct analysis of market trends. Visionary leadership became less important, and management and interpretation took on precedence.

Into the organizational fray came organizational planners, theorists, and consultants who coined the phrase "strategic management." Following hot on the heels of adaptive strategy, this more recent concept works from a slightly different set of assumptions. Although strategic planners assume that one must take into account the vagaries and demands of the environment, unlike adaptive strategists, they neither assume that a decision maker can necessarily accumulate all of the requisite information needed for a decision, nor do they believe that one solution necessarily exists. Either explicitly stated in their work, as does Ellen Chaffee (1984, 1985), or implicitly stated in their discussion, as does George Keller (1983), strategic planners have adopted a view of the world based on *cultural functionalism:* organizations have cultures, and different structures, people, ceremonies, and the like have functions to be maintained if the organization is to function effectively. The task of the leader is to ensure that these functions are effective and efficient for system maintenance. The managers of the system strive for dynamic equilibrium.

Such a theory holds that all organization is created by the interactions of the participants, the institution's history, and an awareness of the present context. Administration, management, leadership, and governance are the four key ingredients of strategic planning that ensure institutional health and renewal. Administration pertains to the effective coordination of activities, and management sees that the right decisions are made. Leadership is charismatic and inspires the "troops," and governance refers to efficient decision making. Unlike adaptive strategists, strategic planners not only need to read their environment, but they need to interpret that environment to a multitude of different constituencies. Organizational leaders manage the institution through communication and design. As with linear and adaptive planning, strategic planning derives from the business world. As Keller notes:

Colleges and universities across the land are realizing that they must manage themselves as most other organizations in society do; they are different and special but not outside the organizational world. Money, markets, competitors, and external forces matter as well as traditions, academic freedom, devotion to ideas and internal preferences. Design is better than drift. . . . Thought is preferable to squabbling (1983, p. 118).

The purpose, then, of strategic management is to "plan the defeat of one's enemies through the effective use of resources" (Keller, 1983, p. 74). A college's enemy might be defined as a competitor who seeks to gain a toehold in one of the institution's markets, or the enemy might be thought of less personally as the market forces that have created the possibility of a fiscal nightmare. In one light it is difficult to disagree with Keller's dramatic language. Who would argue that it is better to squabble than to think? Few individuals want their institution to drift mindlessly.

Robert Birnbaum states the obvious: "Of course, institutions must be aware of their environments, must manage resources prudently, and cannot be indifferent to changing markets without placing themselves in jeopardy" (1988, p. 222). Like Birnbaum, I am hard pressed to see how people desire their institutions not to be aware of environmental threats or engage in resource management. The problem with strategic planning, however, is that Keller has framed the problem as either-or, when actually a variety of options exist. Either an institution plans, or it drifts. Either individuals think logically or they squabble. Such a line of thinking is similar to discussions about effectiveness and efficiency. Who desires ineffectiveness or inefficiency?

The assumption in this text is that we must first have an epistemological understanding of our positions and then develop agendas for action. Strategic planners, however, often go immediately to action plans. They neither consider what a philosophy of education ought to be nor do they develop a philosophy of decision making. The problem is that, as with the manner in which Keller has written about strategic planning, we overlook the assumptions that guide his suggestions. As Nancy Hartsock states, "Theory is always implicit in our activity and . . . includes our understanding of reality. We can either accept the categories given us or we can develop a critical understanding of the world" (1979, p. 57). When we overlook these theoretical assumptions, we implicitly buy into epistemological ideas about the nature of education and community.

From a critical postmodern perspective, however, we see that an investigation of the basic premises of education and decision making enables us to develop alternative epistemological possibilities that move us away from either-or thinking on an action level. Critical postmodernists are neither for inefficiency nor against effectiveness. The fundamental concern with market-oriented decision-making strategies is that they all are epistemologically consistent in terms of how they view the organizational world. That is, although linear, adaptive, and strategic management differ in how individuals ostensibly define the actions of leaders and managers, they are remarkably similar in their epistemological assumptions and outlook.

"The definition of community implicit in the market model," points out Patricia Hill Collins, "sees community as arbitrary and fragile, structured fundamentally by competition and domination" (1991, p. 223). The organization is a market that has goods to sell to consumers. As Keller (1983) noted, academic organizations are like business organizations; economic goals drive the enterprise. And if postsecondary institutions are businesses, then we should rightfully utilize business models to run the organization.

Critical postmodernists offer a dramatically different paradigm to critique and to think about organizational life, one which stresses connection, caring, and difference. Rather than modernist appeals to equilibrium, critical postmodernism seeks to keep institutions in flux so that norms are constantly reconfigured in light of new awareness. Issues of justice and equity rather than economic profit are of central concern. The organization is a community and not a market; we engage in dialogue with one another, and we view organizational activity as intellectual rather than transactual.

Leadership is geared less to management and governance and more toward an intellectual involvement pertaining to justice and equity. As Kenneth Gergen aptly notes, "From the postmodern standpoint, leaders lose their credibility as 'superior knowers' and guiding rationales prove empty" (1991, p. 250). The idea that an individual or group of planners can determine the actions of the community is rejected, for those individuals see the world in a particular, privileged manner. Instead, decisions are shared across groups, and discussion develops within the entire community.

If strategic planning is too bureaucratic or managerial, the idea that decision making is to be shared across groups sounds anarchic. Keller and others may rightfully argue that discussion is fine but decisions often need to be made expeditiously; the idea that decision making is to be consensual provokes visions of academic logjams where nothing gets done. I turn to the case study of Huntsville for one example of how strategic planning itself can result in a logjam. I then return to a discussion of how critical postmodernism might resolve such a dilemma.

STRATEGIC PLANNING AT HUNTSVILLE

Background

Huntsville is a small, private liberal arts college founded more than a hundred years ago in a rural area in the Northeast. Most of the 1,100 students are full-time and reside on campus; many of them are first generation college-goers. There are about seventy-five full-time faculty. As with many other institutions, Huntsville's faculty in many areas is an aging one whose members have begun to retire in increasing numbers.

Eighty percent of those students who apply to Huntsville are accepted, and their average SAT scores are in the 1000 range. The college has garnered some repute for its natural science departments, and students and faculty alike point to the relatively high percentage of the student body who go on to attain graduate degrees as evidence that the college has good programs. The college is coed but neither racially nor ethnically diverse. The student body is drawn primarily from throughout the region. A vast percentage of students qualify for, and receive, financial aid. There are no fraternities or sororities, but there is an extensive array of student activities that everyone is encouraged to join.

When a new president arrived four years ago, the college heaved a collective sigh of relief. In particular, many of the faculty had been demoralized by the previous president's term; they had sought a president who was collegial and believed in the importance of communication and dialogue. "We had a president," commented one individual in a group discussion, "who felt he was the only one to make decisions." "The faculty voice was considerably lessened," added a second. "We were sure to look for someone different, someone who would listen," continued a third. But a fourth person stated, "I've been involved in choosing three presidents here and I must say as I get older I get considerably more pessimistic about democracy. The process isn't right."

If the previous president was at one end of the spectrum in terms of collegiality and dialogue, it is safe to say that the current president occupies the opposite end of that spectrum. Views of the president's style vary. The students are highly complimentary. "The president's a good guy," commented a student. "He's easy to talk to and he knows most of the students' names," said a second. "He goes to the football games, everything. He always cheers the loudest," commented another student.

The faculty also pointed out how the president was very open and easy to talk with, but their comments were not always as positive. "He is easy to talk to, I'll grant that," conceded one faculty member. Another professor said, "I want someone who can make a decision. I'm confused about the vision of Huntsville now, where I wasn't before." A third individual agreed, "The president seems to have so much faith in us that he thinks we can be all things to all people." "His mistakes," added another, "are well-intentioned mistakes. He communicates, sure. But we don't know where we're going. I wish he'd just get on with it." "I disagree," stated another individual who heard the previous comment. "The president has gotten us thinking about what we want to be. He's on the mark." "There seems to be this intense desire to please," concluded another. "You get the feeling that if you engage in dialogue that we like one another, but that's not leadership."

The faculty view of presidential leadership brings into focus the wider topic of decision making in general, and faculty governance in particular. Because the faculty is relatively small, there is no faculty senate with elected representatives. Instead, the faculty meet as a whole body, and the academic dean chairs the meeting. The result is that there is no structural role in the organization that signifies who is a leader among the faculty. "We've had leaders sometimes," reflected a longtime faculty member, "but that was many years ago." "The department chairs might fill the role, but they don't," added another. "What this does is create a vacuum," explained a relative newcomer to the institution. "Everyone speaks up, but no one provides direction."

At the same time, faculty felt they were deeply involved in the governance of the college through the committee structure. "We are all on too many committees," said one individual. Another person explained:

We tend to be here all day. We teach a lot, and then everyone is also called on to serve on different committees. And the committees have subcommittees. The way things get done around here is through people talking with one another on committees. You also find out what is going on in other parts of the college.

Everyone mentioned the dedication of the faculty and the ability to see faculty on a relatively easy basis. The students, in particular, had enthusiastic opinions about the faculty: "They really work hard. I can even go see my advisor on a Friday afternoon, without an appointment," said one student. "The faculty at Huntsville—not everyone, but a lot—want to get to know you," commented another. "I like faculty who don't just read from a lecture, but get involved in and out of the class, and there are a lot here who do that," added another. Still another student continued, "The wall between students and teachers needs to be torn down. People come here because they think they'll be able to find faculty to talk to and you usually do."

The Huntsville faculty do not seem demoralized, but they mention how busy they are. "It's not the teaching, but the committee work that kills you," offered one individual. The confusion about who directs change, and by inference, the role of the faculty and administration, is akin to what was heard at Sherman College. "For an idea to work here," commented one Huntsville individual in a faculty group, "it's got to come from the faculty." A few moments later an individual said, "The president needs to set the parameters, make decisions, and stop forming task forces." When I pointed out the seeming contradiction between the two statements—one saying that the faculty should manage change and the other suggesting it was the president's role—the faculty seemed content to accept both ideas. When I queried other faculty about the contradiction, they too, were comfortable with both ideas. One said, "Our problem has always been this, working out the two sides." Another added, "It's a schizophrenia of desire. We want to run things, but we also know the president should more forcefully set the agenda."

Some faculty also mentioned that the academic dean also had a role, but in general, the comments about the dean's role were relatively few. "We have a first-time president and a first-time dean. They're feeling their way along," said one individual. "The dean can stimulate communication and conversation, but not much else," added a second person. A third person summarized, "The dean's an administrator, not a faculty member. It is a little strange that she runs the faculty meeting, but that's the way it's been."

In some respects, Huntsville recalls college life in the 1950s. Full-time, white, traditional college-aged students live in residence halls and interact with their faculty during class and office hours. Ceremonies and activities such as homecoming abound and are quite important in the life of the community.

Huntsville, however, also faces particular challenges typical of the 1990s. Buildings need to be renovated or built. The library must be upgraded. An aging faculty will gradually retire and need to be replaced. The demand for student financial aid outweighs what can be given. Although faculty governance seems a bit inefficient, there does not seem to be a high degree of animosity or dissatisfaction. In part, this is due to the work of the president, who led a new administrative team into office four years ago and wanted to "provide a clearer image of who we are." We turn to a discussion of the manner in which Huntsville's image was to become clearer.

Strategic Planning at Huntsville

"When I arrived," the president recalled, "I thought we were too fuzzy about what we were about. We had implicit values—'community' appears in our mission statement three times—but we needed greater clarity." The president believed that not only was there a need for a more shared sense of what Huntsville was, but there was also a need for what Huntsville might become. He continued:

In Huntsville's culture, there has always been a view toward outcomes, student outcomes, but we needed to state that more explicitly, more up front. I also want us to move up a notch in quality. I want strength across the curriculum and not just in a few areas. We need a better understanding of the freshman-year experience. And to my surprise, we did not have a facilities plan; we had no idea of a unified picture of the physical plant.

We also do not market ourselves well to the outside. People do not know us. We brought in a consultant who thought our mission statement was "too vanilla." So all these things went along with my reason for starting a strategic plan.

The president's use of both the present and past tense in his statement reflects how the strategic planning process is still not finished. The implementation of strategic planning was threefold. The president named a senior administrator to lead the process. Initially, faculty and staff seemed to buy into the notion. "You know faculty," an individual sighed. "We're task oriented and we like to talk. The president had a task, and it required talk—lots of it. We went along." A "mission" committee composed of faculty, administrators, and students discussed the goals of the college. One individual remembered, "It gave us a common sense of what it meant." Another participant recalled, "People read into it what they wanted, but it was a good start. It said that talking about the mission and goals was important." "The committee was very inclusive, very participatory. It was a broadbrush kind of thing, diagnostic," recalled another individual.

The other two committees addressed internal and external assessment. As described by numerous faculty, the internal assessment committee resembled the kind of committee that colleges create for accreditation reports. Departments were asked to assess their strengths and weaknesses and what kind of resources they needed to improve. One example of a weakness is a liberal arts department in which they rely on part-time faculty to teach, due to either departures or retirements that have not been replaced. The external assessment committee studied the external environment and outlined the opportunities or threats that existed for Huntsville both in the present and future. One opportunity highlighted by the committee was the prediction that by the mid-1990s the declining demographic curve will turn up and the college-age cohort will, in turn, increase. What must be viewed as both a threat and an opportunity was that college-age students desired technologically current educational instruction and support. The problem was the cost needed to develop such classes, and yet the opportunity for creating a new market niche also existed.

Obviously, internal and external assessments may be in conflict or agreement. A liberal arts department may well need an additional faculty member to achieve excellence, but if an external assessment forecasts less need for liberal arts courses and more need for technical coursework, then difficult choices exist. Presumably, a college's mission ought to provide some direction about how to choose among the many difficult options that exist. A liberal arts college where the philosophy department has long been well respected and prominent is probably not well advised to downscale the department in favor of vocational education courses. Again, the point of strategic planning is not simply to adapt to the demands of the environment, but to assess the manifold arenas in which a college operates in order to develop a cohesive and holistic approach to needs changes and innovations.

At Huntsville by the end of the first phase of the strategic planning process, individuals felt good about their respective committees, but they did not yet see how each of the parts provided a sense of direction about where Huntsville should go. "The mission committee and the other ones were okay," said one individual. "It got us going." A second person agreed, "I thought the mission committee did its task relatively well." "I don't like departmental assessments, they seem to always be asking that—what are your strengths and weaknesses," commented another, "but it was an honest attempt."

To most of the faculty, however, the next major step in the process was viewed as a disaster. Logically, the task before the college was to take the various recommendations and analyses of the different committees and incorporate them into a unified document about which areas the college would emphasize and how specific actions might occur. By inference, of course, the college had to decide which departments and programs would not be emphasized.

"We met over the summer and we decided to form five task forces that would outline what was needed to be done," remembered the academic dean. "What a mistake that was," said a faculty member. "First they—primarily administrators—get together over the summer and refine things, and then set up these task forces." Another administrator said, "The tasks were not well defined. We had to prioritize what needed to be done, and one group assumed no resource constraints, and other groups worked within fiscal constraints." "The process," summarized one individual, "was timely and destructive." The president said forthrightly, "I did not exercise enough leadership. It was a mistake." A longtime faculty member explained how the mistake eventually exploded:

It became the biggest disaster I've seen here. It was a very fractious three months. Because people perceived their tasks differently, the reports were different. So we found departments fighting one another. Some said, "Our department needs to be increased because the others have had enough," and then the other departments got angry. There was no follow-up, and the subsequent actions, like adding a member in Geology, or avoiding a discussion about what to do with the foreign languages, made me feel that the whole process was an enormous waste of time that produced more ill will than any sense of where we're going.

"I disagree," countered one professor. "The history department got full support for conducting a national search in the manner in which they desired because of the plan. It had never been done before." "But the same did not happen in other departments—look at the foreign languages," countered another individual. "That's what makes the whole process look whimsical."

"Part of the problem is endemic to Huntsville," explained one professor. "The fellow who was in charge of the whole process was an administrator, and we don't trust him." Another faculty member added, "My sense is the president, vice presidents, and the advisory group have a clear idea of what they want. We don't." A senior administrator agreed in part, "Perhaps the problem is not with what we decided, but how we decided them. The process broke down because there was no natural group leadership of the faculty. We need to work on that and get the planning process back on track."

A faculty member concurred by reflecting on another example of misunderstanding in part due to the structure of communication at Huntsville: "It's akin to the freshman year fiasco where the dean thought she had this neat idea, got money from a foundation, chose the wrong people to get involved and then there was this firestorm of protest from the faculty when we heard about it."

The dean essentially agreed with the analysis by saying, "It was a good idea, but I see now that if you want faculty change they have to believe it. What killed it, or at least stalled it for the time being, was that it was seen as a violation of turf and the way the group was composed." A third individual commented, "We didn't think anything was wrong with the freshman-year experience, and then we found out that something was going to be done. We just put a stop to it. It seemed she wanted the project because her previous institution had one."

In part, each of these issues—the problem of strategic planning, and the initiation of a new project—stems from three misunderstandings that pertain to (1) the overall goals of the college, (2) the kind of information that is gathered to make a decision, and (3) the manner in which that data is disseminated. Ironically, the strategic planning process was supposed to create greater understanding of the college's purpose, yet it seems to have done the opposite. "I don't even know what 'student-oriented outcomes' is, but that's what they say we're about. Where did it come from?" asked one individual. "We've gotten mixed messages," elaborated another person. "We hear that student outcomes and assessment are important, and then it seems that the president wants us to be more [Ivy League]." A new professor said, "I heard that research would be more important from some people, and this was a teaching institution from other people."

"People hide information," commented one professor. "Administrators have different kinds of facts and figures to justify why one department should be enhanced, another should be strengthened, and others should just be maintained." " 'Student outcomes' is supposed to be information-based," commented another, "but so far I haven't seen any of that information." "The process has just broken down," ended one individual. "All this time spent on committees doing this and that, and for what?"

One final point pertains to the purpose of a strategic plan in the minds of the organization's participants. The president pointed out why he wanted such a planning process, but after four years of effort, what were the participants' reflections? "We needed a better marketing tool," said one. "Strategic planning is externally motivated," commented a second. "It's external in the sense that you get the idea that everyone else is doing it and you should too. That accrediting groups want you to do this. It's in the air." "It will help us with our student recruiting," said an advocate. "We have a better idea of which groups have come to Huntsville, and how we need to tap into other groups." Thus, most individuals thought strategic planning was driven either by a new president's desire to better understand the institution for himself or by external demands.

Ironically, other than the individual in charge of the process, it seemed that no one was able to assess strategic planning except in generalized terms. One might think that an institution that committed itself to "student-oriented outcomes" would be able to assess its own actions in specific ways. Yet, the participants either commented in the negative fashion heard above, or in a positive light such as, "If there hadn't been strategic planning, I would have had to make sense of where to go, what to do anyway." "I'm glad we've done it," said another. "It's one of those things you ought to go through every so often. It could have been done better, but the attempt was admirable." "I don't think it's affected me, my office, in any way," concluded a mid-level administrator, "but it's good to talk about institutional image."

DISCUSSION

I stated at the outset of this chapter that the process in which Huntsville was engaged tells us about (1) the nature of academic leadership and strategic planning, (2) the goals of strategic planning, and (3) the manner in which decision making takes place. Before I turn to those three points, it is incumbent upon me to comment on the overall view I have about Huntsville. Although I am suggesting that strategic planning did not work particularly well at Huntsville, the participants do not demonstrate a high degree of conflict or disagreement with one another. It would not be accurate to say that Huntsville is an institution that reflects different constituencies at odds with one another. The negative views that the faculty hold about strategic planning have not frozen attitudes toward the administration to the point that no communication occurs whatsoever. Indeed, morale among administration, faculty, and, in particular, students seems quite high. Yet during my visit, most people did not suggest that strategic planning had helped the process of communication and goal attainment; if anything, strategic planning has hindered the process.

The administration expresses a high degree of goodwill and a desire to include different constituencies in decision making. Although the administration still maintains a strong belief in its ideas and strategic planning, the president and academic dean seem particularly forthright about the mistakes that have been made, and what they should have done both with strategic planning and the idea for changing the freshman-year experience.

Similarly, although I suggest that Huntsville has focused too highly on the external environment, threats do exist that all institutions need to take into account. Markets that once existed may no longer be available to an institution, for example, or opportunities might exist that should be taken.

However, Huntsville's constituents seem to have engaged in strategic planning not for themselves but for others. My central concern here is particularly with such an institution's focus. How might an educational institution remain competitive and communicate an aura of quality to external constituencies and at the same time engage in processes that highlight intergroup communication and solidarity?

Critical Leadership and Strategic Planning

At first glance, it may seem paradoxical that the faculty wanted the president to make decisions while, at the same time, they also believed that any substantive decisions had to come from the faculty. From a critical perspective, however, academic leadership in strategic planning enables different constituencies to set the framework for decision making and to develop those decisions. At Huntsville, such actions are difficult, if not impossible. The structure of the organization has developed so that administrators control—however benevolently—information and communicative processes.

There are instrumental actions that might be taken; a faculty member might be put in charge of strategic planning, for example, and somehow the professoriate needs an academic structure through which they have a voice. Whether that voice comes from the chair of a faculty senate or from a presidential cabinet that includes a chair of the faculty is irrelevant; what matters is that faculty have a voice and structure that is distinct from the administration's. From a postmodern perspective, decentralization enables distinctly different voices to arise, and from a critical perspective, decentralization enables oppositional voices to speak.

Huntsville's administration acknowledges the importance of communication, yet what appears to be lacking is a unified perspective about how communication and, hence, decisions best occur. Any small organization has a high degree of informal dialogue and contact, and such is the case at Huntsville. Huntsville's constituents also believe they have an overabundance of formalized opportunities for communication through their committee structure. Strategic planning (and now preparation for an accreditation visit) creates another layer of committee meetings. From the data developed here, I am not convinced that such an elaborate committee structure is in the best interests of either the individuals involved in the process or for decision making in general. To be sure, committees serve various functions as symbolic entities, as overseeing bodies, and as disseminators of information. However, committees also serve to reinforce bureaucratic structures and often have two destructive consequences. First, decisions that might be made in a relatively short time frame often take countless weeks of discussion. Second, individuals who must attend committee meetings do not become engaged in intellectual tasks but bureaucratic ones. The strategic planning process at Huntsville is a good example.

Huntsville's faculty and administrators spent countless hours discussing a mission statement and found when they finished that they had arrived back from where they had started. No one can point to how Huntsville's 1990s mission statement has changed Huntsville, and the statement remains "too vanilla," in one person's words. The hours spent in meetings eventually devolved the activities to a few individuals who wrote the documents and the others who critiqued the pages, to change words from "enhance" to "strengthen," for example.

The point is not to deride the process, but rather to suggest that academic leadership ought to present a more forceful intellectual presence so that the community engages with one another not in bureaucratic forms where internecine fights eventually erupt over terms, but rather the community participates in a process in which they are able to speak from their own personal experiences about the life of the community. Henry Giroux has commented on the kind of leadership I am suggesting. He states that a transformative intellectual "exercises forms of intellectual and pedagogical practice that attempt to insert teaching and learning directly into the political sphere by arguing that schooling represents both a struggle for meaning and a struggle over power relations" (1988a, p. 174). Such a definition suggests a leader distinctly different from a strategic manager concerned with marketing and effectiveness. Rather than moving the organization toward equilibrium, the individual strives to understand differences and encourages reflexive discourse aimed at orienting the organization toward agape.

A leader of the kind I am suggesting assumes two contradictory stances. On the one hand, the individual sets an intellectual, rather than a bureaucratic, tone for the institution. On the other hand, the leader creates the conditions by which diverse dialogues about the nature of the institution take place. Thus, the leader is both a listener who voices and a participant who offers a particular view. Such a view of leadership is distinctly different from the old-fashioned view of a leader as a "great man" who sets the direction of the institution, or of leadership as a synonym for management. Instead, the leader views his/her task as an intellectual process that necessitates ongoing multivocal dialogue.

Strategic Goals

Rightfully or not, many in Huntsville's community believed that the goals of strategic planning were to develop marketing tools for external constituencies. The ultimate goal—student-oriented outcomes—was one that will enable Huntsville to communicate how well they are doing to the outside world. The strength of such an approach is easily understandable. Educational foundations appreciate knowing that a college has increased student learning from one point to another. Parents and students like to know that the college of their choice is increasing in quality along several different dimensions.

My concern in this regard, however, is what we lose by concentrating so heavily on developing goals that are understandable to external constituencies. As I noted in the previous chapter, Americans in the late twentieth century seem to have an almost obsessive desire to quantify different issues and topics. A college or university ought to be able to satisfy the demands of different external constituencies about how quality is judged. Yet such a task should not be the work of the university community, but rather should be assigned to an individual involved with university relations.

From a critical postmodern perspective, the fabric of an educational community is the members' fealty to a discourse concerned with the life of the intellect. "Agape enjoins one to identify with the neighbor's point of view," notes Gene Outka, "to try imaginatively to see what it is for him to live the life he does. . . . The other's right to assume a point of view different from one's own is also affirmed" (1972, p. 311). For such discussions to occur, we create committees that concentrate on the development of fellowship among one another, rather than on how to satisfy the perceived demands of external groups. Education is a process that ought to involve dialogue about one's place in society and within our own communities. To develop such a community, we necessarily raise questions about what kind of community we want to be. And these questions are not worked out by way of formalized goals, but rather they are enacted on a daily basis among one another.

Decision Making in a Postmodern World

Educational organizations are not business organizations, and we ought not to be forced into trying to become such. By that I mean that a for-profit business organization ultimately assesses itself through an analysis of a profit margin. Colleges and universities should not be made to think that students are markets that need to be tapped or products that need to be improved; such assumptions lose sight of what education is and insult virtually all of the constituencies involved in the educational process.

Strategic management and other functionalist theories of organizations are, as Robert Merton noted more than a quarter of a century ago, "oriented toward the needs of management" (1968, p. 625). The problems chosen as well as the focus of their solutions have developed from a managerial frame of decision making. Many alternate frames exist, and the one utilized here is based on critical postmodernism. Such an approach focuses on the structural relations of power in the organization and on how reality is constructed. Rather than assume that the purpose of organizational life is to act rationally and achieve stasis, we investigate how to develop dialogue among often competing interests. Although I will expand on these ideas in Chapter 7, I set the stage, so to speak, with five approaches to decision making: (1) structure, (2) hierarchy, (3) committees, (4) pedagogy and structure, and (5) comparative awareness.

Structure. The interests of faculty and administration are not always alike. Administrators may have greater needs for dealing with external constituencies, and faculty may have more desire to improve the relations within the classroom. Administrators may think of how they can reduce the costs of sizable blocs of resources—such as faculty salaries—and faculty may resist paying a senior administrator an income that the board of trustees feels is justified.

I raise these specific examples not because they are issues at Huntsville, but simply to point out that when we speak of a "community of difference," we are assuming that different individuals and groups have unique interests, and, of consequence, an organization needs to incorporate those interests through a structure that enables voices to develop. An example at Huntsville would be the creation of a faculty senate that is run by the faculty and develops an agenda distinct from that of the administration.

Reduce Hierarchy. To a certain extent, postmodern organizations thrive on contradictions, and at first glance, this suggestion seems to contradict the first point. I am suggesting that administrative and faculty roles be less clearly defined so that all individuals seize decision-making responsibility rather than let it reside primarily in one arena. Even though decision making becomes blurred in a postmodern world, different groups do not have to have unique structural entities. In essence, postmodern organizations have a twofold task: (1) of creating arenas where individuals who have distinct interests may congregate, debate, recommend, and decide, and (2) of developing a sense of community where decisions are based on the debate of the whole.

Such a portrait suggests that faculty become involved in areas such as student life and, conversely, that student affairs administrators have something to say about curricular matters. This point pertains particularly to senior administrators. Often we find that "administrators administer"; I am suggesting not only that decision making be shared, but also that roles become intertwined. To be sure, we often think that faculty have a role in governance, but we also need to reinsert administrators and staff into the teaching and learning process. Such a suggestion implies that at a teaching institution everyone will be involved in teaching.

Temporary Committees. If the life of the community is geared toward the intellect, then we need to focus our time more centrally on intellectual tasks. Just like at countless institutions, at Huntsville individuals complained of the overwhelming amount of committee work that often produced few, if any, tangible results. Again, a contradiction exists with this suggestion in comparison with my point about structure, for the idea here is to reduce the committee structure and develop a more fluid decision-making style.

Committees might develop specific charges and meet as quickly as possible in order to dispense with an issue. Standing college committees often have leisurely agendas and meet once a month throughout the academic year, and the committee's apparent purpose is of little more than symbolic import. Yet such symbols all too often depress people about the meaninglessness of their input. Instead, why not create committees that "go out of business" within a very short time frame rather than debate issues seemingly ad nauseam?

Obviously, certain decisions cannot be made in a month's time, but as anyone knows who serves on college committees such as the ones discussed at Huntsville, the vast majority of decisions are not so involved that they necessitate a year's worth of consideration. We do ourselves a disservice both instrumentally and ideologically by discussing the vast array of academic items at a snail's pace. Instrumentally, decisions get bogged down; more importantly, individuals remove themselves from committees—either in body or in mind—when they feel that the tasks before them are trivial.

Pedagogy and Structure. If some committees are trivial, others deserve more prominence. If some tasks can be solved in a brief moment, others require concerted, sustained inquiry. The debate that rages in academe about curriculum and interdisciplinary foci demands more structured attention from college communities than it is presently given. Again, committees that meet over minute items once a month are not necessarily able to engage in the sort of dialogue that I am suggesting here.

Huntsville spoke in broad brushstrokes about its mission and about how to increase departmental allotments. Such discussions are the norm. I am suggesting, however, that individuals involve one another in the most intense dialogues over the nature of learning. Outside speakers might be brought in, and readings might be included. The point is the process. Rather than a task that has a goal of deciding which department to increase and which to decrease, we need to rediscover how to speak intellectually to one another. I appreciate that faculty and administrators are too busy; in large part, my suggestion about reducing trivial committee work feeds into this suggestion.

Community does not simply happen; we need to enable mutual dialogues of respect and difference to take place. To meet one another in an intellectual dialogue demands that we have the time and desire. At present most faculties have neither the time nor the desire. To create the stimulus for change demands leadership of the kind that the Huntsville faculty implicitly suggested. The president of an institution needs to redirect his/her energies from that of an external agent to that of one who is a transformative intellectual willing and able to foment dialogue across constituencies.

Comparative Awareness. I offer yet another contradiction. However strong an organization's culture and ideology may be, there are times when such cultural strength breeds insularity. We must constantly remind ourselves that previous ideas of community often based themselves on notions that absented women, people of color, and others from the community. A postmodern version of organizational culture demands a comparative awareness of other institutional cultures—their structures, interactions, and ideologies.

As I noted in the previous chapter, to the extent that the community's individuals can have others visit the campus or that they can visit campuses themselves, they will be able not simply to learn about another culture but to reflect on their own. I am suggesting something different from faculty attending a conference to present a paper. Although helpful, such conferences speak more to a faculty's disciplinary culture than to institutional culture. Instead, an institution will be improved if individuals are able to spend a day or two at another campus and then report on what they found in an open forum; institutions might even develop a faculty exchange program through which faculty spend a semester teaching at another institution. Such a suggestion does not have to involve vast sums of resources, and the potential for self-learning in the community is great.

Finally, let me reemphasize that I am not suggesting that we cease to consider whether the organization is acting in a manner that is both efficient and effective. Countless nonprofit organizations have stream-lined their activities by learning from profit-making businesses. Postsecondary institutions also have been aided by consultants who have helped them tap into markets that the college otherwise would not have considered. However, such actions ought to be viewed for what they are—incremental adjustments to improve the ultimate task of the institution. And the ultimate task is the manner in which we engage one another as educational citizens.

Chapter Six

Structure and Knowledge: Building a University

What might a university for the twenty-first century look like if we were free to choose its design? This text has studied institutions encumbered with difficult histories and cultures that struggle to maintain their integrity in a context presently fraught with trouble. Without such a history, without any troublesome preexisting conditions, how might an institution be configured to meet more adequately the needs of the postmodern age? These are not merely idle questions, for, in some locales, postsecondary institutions are being built, and the individuals involved in the construction of these organizations must grapple with a host of such questions.

California State University at San Marcos is but one example of a small number of institutions that have been started not in the economic boom times of the 1960s, but rather in the post-1970s era of fiscal belt-tightening. As with the discussion of Deep Springs College, a discussion of San Marcos is important not merely for those individuals at other institutions that are in the throes of being born, but also for organizational participants in the multitude of institutions that have existed for decades, if not centuries. An institution such as San Marcos offers an example as to how older institutions also might change.

What are those problems that existing colleges and universities have that a new institution might avoid? Are there structures or relationships that a new institution might implement that would help organizational participants in older institutions overcome the myriad of problems they currently encounter? Creative answers to these questions have the potential to point a new direction to academe, and one may plausibly argue that such a direction is most often set by new institutions that, presumably, are relatively free to determine their course.

Accordingly, in this chapter I will discuss three themes. First, I will consider the background pertaining to the creation of San Marcos and suggest the parameters that surround an institution even prior to its creation. I will then highlight the tension between institutional structure and the definition of knowledge, considering how such definitions determine the teaching and learning process. I will conclude with a discussion about diversity and difference and how twenty-first-century institutions might more forcefully confront these issues in light of the efforts currently underway at San Marcos.

BREAKING NEW GROUND: THE BEGINNING

The desire to build additional postsecondary institutions in California in general, and in southern California in particular, began in the late 1960s. Efforts were initially resisted, but eventually the influx of people and economic development of the counties north of San Diego necessitated serious consideration of a new institution. Throughout the 1980s, the outline of what would become California State University (CSU)–San Marcos took shape in the CSU state system office as well as in arenas such as the legislature and the nearby institution of San Diego State University. By 1988 the decision had been made to create a new institution.

Originally, the plan for the campus was that it would eventually reach twenty-five thousand students, with ten thousand of that total reached before the end of the decade. However, the California state university system is in the throes of the most serious fiscal crisis it has ever faced. Indeed, there have been and will continue to be in the forseeable future dramatic fluctuations in state planning for the campus. Recent predictions are for a considerably smaller institution than the original twenty-five thousand students, and some individuals have even predicted the eventual closing of the institution if the state economy does not improve.

Nevertheless, the state has bought land for the campus and construction has begun in stages. In the meantime, the university works out of efficient, new office space close to the site of the hoped-for future university. The present FTE (full-time equivalent) enrollment approaches one thousand students, most of whom transferred from two local community colleges, and faculty growth has doubled every year. The university will offer bachelor's and master's degrees.

The president and executive vice president assumed control of the institution in July 1989, and eleven "founding faculty" arrived two months later to help plan the university. These thirteen individuals and a few consultants spent the next twelve months in extensive consultation with one another about the nature of the institution. "We met every day around a table," commented one person. "I'd never seen anything like it." "We shared personal experiences," added another, "and we listed what we did and didn't want." "It was intellectually exciting because we weren't bound by academic areas," reminisced a third. "There weren't fiefdoms. There was just a tremendous amount of energy. I was able to talk to people in areas that I normally didn't talk with," concluded a fourth.

Although a tremendous amount of excitement and enthusiasm existed, there were also rough spots along the way. "I should have spoken up more," said one person of color. "I'm a typical minority, I guess. Very observant. Very aware. But we won't talk about it. We keep it inside. On the other hand, if you ask, we'll tell you. I wish I had been more vocal." Another person added, "People came from everywhere, and that was part of the problem. The CSU people kept telling us we couldn't do something because the CSU system wouldn't allow it." A CSU person pointed out the same point from a different perspective: "I hate to see us develop something and go down the road and have the plug pulled. Knowing what I do about the system, I know we have to do certain things, and it was not always easy to make others see that." Another individual added an additional difference among the founding faculty, "I've gotten frozen into a mold, partly because of the system, but also because of rivalries across areas, across colleges. It's normal political infighting for resources." Virtually everyone at the institution mentioned the same reason for wanting to work there. "I know someone else who did something like this, and they said it's an experience they'd never forget," said one person. Another added, "I wanted to get in on the ground floor. To create something." And a third: "I thought I'd have the chance to build an institution. It was exciting, a once in a lifetime opportunity." Finally, a fourth: "I wanted to establish the paradigm rather than have it set for me." The assumption for each of these people was that in one way or another they were going to create something new and different.

To be sure, the location in southern California was also appealing, but faculty who were attracted to building an institution were different from the norm, for such an effort takes a tremendous amount of energy and time. Perhaps in their differences, they were similar. That is, the faculty sought out San Marcos not merely because they wanted to move to a pleasant area or to another position, but because they desired to create a new institution. Other than that similarity, however, the founding faculty and subsequent hires have had little in common. The president outlined his initial hiring plan, which has not changed:

We find people from everywhere and tell them to duke it out. We purposefully chose people from across institutions. We wanted a deliberate mix. No good old boys. No prior allegiances. We get the best individuals, the best chemist, the best mathematician, and let them go. We want conscious decisions. Everything is up for grabs.

Consequently, the founding faculty and subsequent hires have arrived from a patchwork quilt of American higher education—Stanford and Ball State, Harvard Medical School and Waukesha County Technical College. Arguably, the current faculty may come from the most diverse academic backgrounds of any faculty in the United States. Further, the faculty is also diverse in terms of race and gender. Whereas less than 30 percent of the composite faculty nationally is composed of women, San Marcos approaches parity. Although the national average hovers around 10 percent for faculty who are an ethnic minority, and the CSU system as a whole is less than 20 percent, San Marcos has more than 40 percent of its faculty who are people of color.

Diversity has created two dilemmas. On the one hand, because individuals have such different academic backgrounds, it appears that the institution lacks an educational philosophy. On the other hand, the racial and gender diversity has brought about "creative tension." Both dilemmas are being worked out by way of the discussions and actions of the organization's participants as they construct—sometimes literally—the institution. What follows is a discussion first of philosophic diversity and then of racial/gender diversity.

Philosophic Diversity

The president referred to his hiring plan as a way for faculty of diverse opinions to "duke it out." Certainly the system had set in place specific requirements prior to the president's arrival, and he added requirements. The university, for example, was certified to offer majors in English and business administration but not engineering or computer science. The president initially looked for faculty who were "senior" rather than "junior." And too, the president and staff in the CSU system office assumed particular external demands. As one person explained:

We have lots of external constraints. Students expect particular things. We're a demand-driven institution because we're part of the system. We can't be experimental like Evergreen State or Santa Cruz were. We read what our market wants, and we have to respond. The academy also says certain things—about promotion and tenure, for example—that makes us think a particular way.

This comment underscores the restrictions that existed even prior to the time that the founding faculty sat down together to "duke it out." Presumably, most senior faculty—regardless of the institution from which they have come—will have a greater affiliation to their discipline than newer faculty. The assumption that "we can't be experimental" frames dialogue in a manner different from discussions that begin "we must be experimental." Offering majors in English and business administration—or engineering or computer science, for that matter—frames academic discourse in a manner fundamentally different than if individuals had been hired to a pedagogic plan that assumed interdisciplinarity. My point here is not that one framework is right and the other one is wrong, but rather I am trying to delineate how academic structures and definitions of knowledge are set even prior to initial discussions about curriculum.

Curiously, given the framework that has been outlined, we then find a philosophic diversity that highlights even further academic structure and discourse that recreate traditional modes of defining knowledge and curriculum. "There are two cultures on campus," explained one person. "Some people think we can't be like other campuses, we need to be different—interdisciplinary—and other people think we need to build disciplines and departments." Another person continued, "Some of us as founding faculty came here expecting to be leaders, to help build up our areas." A person newer to the campus added, "There's sort of a split between the founding faculty and the new faculty. The founding faculty acted like they were the ones in charge, and we didn't come here for that." "People fall back on what they know," said another individual. "And what we know comes from all kinds of institutions, so we have large disagreements." "This place is at times quite dysfunctional," admitted one person. "We're new, and since we're new, everything's out in the open for all to see."

The consequences of differing opinions are perhaps best exemplified by the mission statement. The president noted, "A committee fought and argued over it. It's not slick, it's purposefully one page that you can pick up, but you can't ignore it. It's meant to engage you, to engage us and help define who we are and who we will be." The mission statement, however, represents a philosophy that one might find on any number of campuses in the United States—even at Huntsville or Sherman. The university "offers excellence in undergraduate and graduate education"; "upholds a high level of academic scholarship in research and teaching;" "demands fairness and decency of all persons." The only explicitly unique aspect of the mission statement is the university's desire for an international perspective that addresses "the global community," yet even that statement is open to multiple interpretations on the part of the organization's participants. One individual, for example, thought the manner in which the institution's commitment to the global community should be enacted was through the curriculum; another individual suggested that the composition of the faculty and students defined multiculturalism; and another person spoke of the "global community" in terms of internships and work-study programs.

Not surprisingly, when asked what the mission of the institution was, individuals offered a variety of quite different responses. A student commented, "We'll be Stanford South, just like Stanford." A faculty member concluded, "We're a state school, like other state schools." "We'll be like a medical school in terms of the education we deliver," offered another individual. "We'll be more practice oriented." "Structurally, we won't be different. I'm not really sure," responded a fourth person. A fifth person continued, "I think we'll be known for our teaching." A sixth person summarized, "We'll be diverse. That's what's different about us, our diversity."

The respondents' comments were interesting because of the general manner and tone in which they were expressed. Their comments about the mission of the institution are what countless other individuals might say about their own institutions. At other institutions, however, individuals often do not expect their mission statement to define the overarching ideology of the organization; rather, participants find purpose in history and organizational culture. At San Marcos, however, as an institution without a history, the mission statement is a document that supposedly defines activities and meaning for the participants. A sense of resignation, or perhaps disappointment, pervaded most of the comments made when individuals were asked about the mission. In particular, when asked what the institution would be like in the year 2000, the participants registered a sense of melancholia.

"I guess we'll be like everybody else," said one individual. "I didn't come here for that, though." "Ninety percent of what we do will be comparable to other schools," said another. "I don't know if we'll be different. It's hard to predict," agreed a faculty member. "What we'll see and what I'd like to see are probably different," said another. "It will probably be 'business as usual' a perpetuation of the system." "We still can change, but it depends on the collective will," summarized a final person.

These comments highlight that a structure of knowledge was in place prior to the founding faculty's first meeting and that the faculty's philosophic diversity reaffirmed implicit norms of a public state university. Thus, rather than engage in dialogues where the nature of organizational reality was up for grabs, the participants have had to react to the ideological norms established by the state. Perhaps the most potent example of what different philosophies portend in the daily life of the institution pertains to the promotion-and-tenure process. When asked what they would tell a young scholar about tenure, faculty characteristically responded with a wealth of opinions. "Teaching will be important," said one faculty member. "It's very undefined, very unclear," said another. "We say teaching is important, but we just use student evaluations," added another. One faculty member pointed out how San Marcos is similar to other state universities: "It will be standard—like other schools. Teaching, research, and service. Right now, lots of service." "Our teaching is great today," added another person. "We have such small classes that we give good attention to students. But I suppose that will change. It's too bad. I don't know what we'll be like. The budget plays such a big role." Another person downplayed teaching and highlighted research, "I'd say to get your publications going. People say service a lot these days, but anybody can do service. The purpose of a university is to contribute to knowledge—research." Another person partially concurred, "Teaching is 50 percent. Individuals should also do research that will lead to publication in peer-reviewed journals. Quality, not quantity, is what I'd like to see."

Two thoughts arise about the multitude of opinions expressed here. On the one hand, one cannot emphasize enough that San Marcos is a brand-new institution, and to a certain extent, uncertainty about a policy or the future is bound to occur. As one individual said:

You don't know how much effort it takes to start a university. Sure we need to talk about teaching, about evaluation of teaching. We need to talk about many things. But there's no time. We are all stretched to the limit, constantly in meetings, on committees, trying to get things up and running and teach at the same time. I've come into the office every day I've been here. Vacations. Weekends. All my free time. It's very stressful.

On the other hand, such diversity of opinion seems to preclude a sense of binding organizational ethos around a common theme or topic. Although the philosophic diversity evidenced at San Marcos is a step toward postmodern engagement, the powerful norms of the state seem to have precluded discussions through which reality is actually able to be constructed by the participants. Those involved are able to create some changes, but these configurations are akin to what countless other institutions undertake rather than what the participants themselves assumed they would be able to do when they first arrived. San Marcos will not become what Burton Clark once defined as a "distinctive college" (1980), where individuals invest in the institution because of their deep beliefs about organizational purpose. Deep Springs, Reed, and Hampshire Colleges are distinctive colleges that have unique identities that force a particular institutional image and, consequently, specific forms of institutional, curricular, and pedagogic action.

Hence, the concerns about San Marcos reflect common concerns faced by the multitude of other institutions in the United States: What constitutes good teaching? What should be the role of the faculty member? What should be the role of the institution vis-à-vis the state? Unlike Sherman or Huntsville, however, San Marcos is able to approach these questions without the trappings of an organizational past or even a present context that defines how such decisions are made. Indeed, in part, how the decisions are made is as important as any specific decision itself. San Marcos has the possibility of answering such questions in a manner akin to Deep Springs, Huntsville, or Sherman, and as we have seen, the forum for answering those questions has influenced the eventual answers.

What is curious about such questions at San Marcos is that faculty said that they came to the institution to be different, "to get in on the ground floor." Yet they seemed to have reinvented an institution remarkably similar to its predecessors. Again, the situation at San Marcos leads us to consider the following questions: If someone asked for a new postsecondary institution to be built, what would it look like? How would it be formed? Who would populate it? We turn to a discussion of the San Marcos faculty who have been engaged in trying to answer these very questions.

Racial and Gender Diversity

The singular most important difference between the San Marcos faculty and faculty at other postsecondary institutions pertains to ethnic and gender composition. As noted, San Marcos is presently well above national and state averages. The diversity of the faculty has created, in the words of one individual, a "creative tension." Indeed, the pluralism of the faculty may become the defining factor of what the institution is in the year 2000. As one individual explained:

Most universities are struggling to decide how to bring culture and diversity to the table. We've brought it to the table, and the truly interesting question is how will that have made a difference. Will we be different because we have created a diverse population? We may not be that much different, but the processes we use to get where we are going may be quite different.

Another individual concurred: "It's very different here—meeting styles, management styles, decision-making styles. There's conflict sometimes, but up to now it's been a good tension." "We fight about things I never thought about before," admitted one individual. "Like the names of courses. And should we decide things formally or informally. I've always been informal, and now I'm told that that's not right." "We'll be different because the people are different," argued another individual. "People may not realize it, but diversity means more than just that faculty of color are here." Another person continued, "I've seen people leave meetings, go out of the room mad, because of what someone said. But we always get back together. It's just that we're not used to different ways of doing things." "We're at an advantage," concurred another person, "because we don't have to debate about diversity, to decide if it's good or not—the p.c. [political correctness] thing. We need to decide, however, what's the next step." A dean elaborated:

If we don't continue to attract a diverse faculty, we'll fail. We have a commitment as a university, and that is something that everyone is aware of. But there will be a very different way we will have to deal with things here. Until we realize that business will be conducted differently, we won't understand it. This has to be built campuswide, and as we grow it will become more difficult, more of a challenge. It is also our opportunity.

The twin diversities—of philosophy and people—create a climate that most would say is both exciting and stressful. "We hired faculty with different dreams," said one individual, "and such diversity can be a danger." "There's a dialectic of competing visions," added another. A founding faculty member summarized, "It's like a pledge class in a fraternity. We've fought tooth and nail. It's very stressful and it demands trust." A newer faculty member agreed, "Faculty morale is a big issue and we need to confront it. Sometimes there's a sense of a lack of achievement. We never take a breath." "It's all part of stages of development," added another faculty member. "My concern is that we need to talk and if we don't we're in trouble."

ORGANIZATIONAL SCAFFOLDING

The manner in which the organizational participants have spoken about the mission and purpose of San Marcos, and the parameters outlined by the state system, suggest both an organizational structure and assumptions about knowledge. If we return to the initial portrait of the eleven founders and the president and vice president convened around a table, we may analyze it for what it tells us about the way in which decisions are made and about initial beliefs about knowledge. We see, for example, neither students nor community representatives around the table, which implies that those who will make decisions are faculty, administrators, and the invisible hand of the state.

The faculty come from professional schools or traditional disciplines such as English, business, and education, which suggests that knowledge resides within specific disciplinary contexts and awaits to be discovered. Another way to have chosen faculty, for example, would have been to select only individuals involved in cross-disciplinary studies. Still another way would have been to choose individuals because of their superb teaching skills rather than their academic areas. My point here is not to suggest that one hiring schema is better than another, but that the plan one employs ultimately affects the decisions made about how knowledge is defined, structured, and taught.

Most individuals portray the president as a facilitator who enabled discussion to occur, rather than as someone who set an agenda. Indeed, during the first year, the founding faculty felt a sense of ownership that many of them feel they have subsequently lost. "Part of it was we were so small," reminisced one founder. "We all had Thanksgiving at the president's house. It was almost like a family." And like a family, they had their share of fights and disagreements. Yet individuals assumed that they had the prerogative to make decisions. The organizational structure—composed of thirteen individuals—provided for quality and consensus.

As the institution grew, however, the individuals needed to decide how best to govern. "It was interesting," reflected one person, "how many different ideas people had about how to put things together. But then we found out that the system office said they had money for three deans, so we created three colleges—education, business administration, and arts and sciences." The creation of entities such as "colleges" has far-reaching implications for the manner in which individuals interact with one another as well as for how courses get constructed. "We're in different buildings now," said one individual. "It's just common that we don't see one another as much anymore." The individual went on to bemoan the fact that when the campus is built, the separation among the various colleges and departments will be even greater. Interestingly, the current geographic distance between the faculty in education and the faculty in business or arts and sciences is a few hundred feet; but nonetheless when faculty saw each other every day around a table, moving to different buildings created an intensely different experience.

It has become commonplace in academia to speak about the "social construction of knowledge." San Marcos is an example of the architectural implications of such an idea, for San Marcos has geographically placed individuals according to traditionally defined parameters of knowledge, and as some have already observed, such placement affects who one interacts and, ultimately, works with on research and teaching. Consider the difference between a faculty such as that at Deep Springs where everyone sees one another constantly throughout the day. Simply stated, if individuals complete their work by informal as well as formal interactions, then it seems incumbent for us to consider the informal community mechanisms that enable individuals to come together irrespective of academic background or departmental focus.

Further, colleges suggest boundaries of knowledge. Faculty work toward achieving accreditation in their unit, and they seek resources to bolster and expand their specific area. "Competition started right away," remembered one individual. "One group said they needed more faculty immediately, and they had to take it from somewhere." "Resources are tight, especially now. So we have people thinking about how they can increase their area. It's quite normal, actually," said another person. A third person added, "People want to build their departments up."

The creation of departments is also underway. Although some individuals seek to resist departments, it seems inevitable to many individuals that as the institution grows, departments will be logical additions. "Perhaps we don't need them this year," explained one person, "but we have people now filling the role of department chairs. They just have a different title. In five years, we'll all have departments." By creating structures such as colleges and departments, San Marcos has begun the process whereby individuals will identify with their specific unit rather than with the university.

We find such evidence in responses to questions about what the institution will be like in the year 2000: "My department will be stronger," or "We'll have Ph.D.'s in our program," or "Hopefully, our curriculum in business will be stronger, different, from what it is now." Such statements suggest that the individual's identity derives from the local level rather than at the more encompassing level where an overarching institutional ideology might help explicitly determine how individuals act.

One might wonder if it is possible to maintain a dual affiliation—both to the institution and to one's college or department. The point, however, is not necessarily that they are in competition with one another but that a person generally becomes socialized and maintains an identity with a finite number of associations. Where, one asks, does an individual identify? Where does someone learn how to act? Past research has shown that when an explicit organizational ideology is absent, members find and create meaning on the levels through which they interact daily—in their programs, departments, or colleges.

It surely does not take an organizational theorist to posit that structure influences behavior. If an institution does not have a development office, it seems unlikely that it will raise large sums of money from donors. If a college does not have an athletic department, then organized sports are probably not a priority. Similarly, if an institution is structured by departments, then a particular way of defining knowledge and of group interaction has been set. I am not suggesting that one particular structure is correct; any number of configurations exist with regard to development offices and athletic departments. Yet one wonders if traditionally designed academic departments are the optimal configuration for an institution entering the twenty-first century.

The last fifty years have created dramatic changes in the way we think about knowledge. Or rather, as Clifford Geertz has noted, "The refiguration of social theory represents a sea change in our notion not so much of what knowledge is but of what it is we want to know" (1983, p. 34). If one concurs with Geertz, then we must at least question whether the best structure for investigating "what we want to know" is the academic department. I suspect any number of possible responses exist, and again, each structure in part determines what the institution wants to know, and ultimately, what it will find.

The elaboration of the organization's structure also has moved power toward the administration. "I don't know how it happened," complained one individual. "We moved too fast. In a very short time we lost faculty voice and put it in administrative authority." A second person concurred, "We probably have put too many resources into administration too fast. It's understandable. We have many needs and they all can't be met. But administrators administer—that's what they're paid to do, and when that happens, faculty power erodes. It has to." It ought to be stressed that in general everyone was highly complimentary of the new administration; indeed, people did not dispute that the administration was hardworking. Instead, individuals expressed concern about the evolving relationship between administration and faculty. As one individual said:

We're growing so fast, so continuously. I don't want to see the AVP [academic vice president] isolate himself, or see the deans form a group away from the rest. They need to make judicious additions to staff, sure, but I hope it's not like at so many other places. We don't need a big divide between faculty and administration. Ernie, Dick, and Rich [all administrators] all teach and that's impressive. I know how hard that is and I appreciate it. I hope we don't fall into hardened roles—'you do this' and 'I do that' sort of thing.

Regardless of the hope that the institution not develop "hardened roles," it seems inevitable that San Marcos will move in that direction. Any new institution needs to develop routines and procedures that enable individuals to work in an efficient manner. However, what the preceding comment is actually referring to is not organizational efficiency, but rather, to the way in which people relate to one another. And I am suggesting that structure in large part also helps determine individual relationships.

As I noted at Huntsville, one plausible configuration for an institution of the twenty-first century is to collapse relationships so that administrators and faculty become intertwined in the teaching and learning process. San Marcos is a good example of an institution that has begun that way because no strict differentiation existed between faculty and administration at the outset. From a critical postmodern perspective, we assume that San Marcos's participants exist in a dialectical relationship with their structure whereby they create a structure that, in turn, shapes human interaction. At this point, however, it appears that the structure has had a much more pervasive influence than the participants would have hoped; indeed, a central challenge is to consider how individuals might organize so that they are able to create dialogues about what they desire rather than merely conform to the demands of the state.

The role the state plays in framing structure has already been mentioned. Obviously, that San Marcos is part of a state university system has set certain boundaries. Yet interestingly, up until the revelations about the draconian budget cutbacks, most individuals did not look to the state system as an impediment or as a straight jacket that predetermined the nature of organizational discourse; rather, individuals looked to the interpretations of other individuals as the problem. "When we go to the office and tell them what we want to do," explained a person, "their first response is 'No, you have to do it this way.' But eventually we get things worked out." "I've been told we couldn't do something," said a founding faculty member, "but then I found out that I could if I did it a particular way. The guy who told me had just been wrong." "There are requirements, sure. But there's much more room to do things than I imagined," agreed another professor. The president said, "At the upper level, they are very supportive. We need to keep in constant dialogue with them, let them get to know us. They have given us quite a bit of autonomy—but it takes a lot of explaining."

Obviously, a state's economic demise is another matter entirely. During the writing of this text, California policymakers have suggested cuts in institutional budgets up to 33 percent. Some individuals have maintained that San Marcos would receive one more year's worth of funding and then they would decide its long-term future. The fiscal future is very uncertain in California. If such dramatic cutbacks take place, they compromise virtually everything that the institution has set out to do—the clientele they serve, the extracurricular activities they are able to provide, and the courses and faculty that account for the institution. Like earthquakes, massive budget reductions of the kind that have been discussed send shocks of change through institutional life. I will return to this point in Chapter 7 by offering some preliminary comments about how public institutions might best respond to their ever-decreasing fiscal allotments from the state. For the present context, however, we have seen that San Marcos has been able to function by being in constant dialogue with the state.

Indeed, most everything San Marcos has done has taken "a lot of explaining." A new institution demands a wealth of time on the part of the organization's participants simply to get up and running. We have come a far way from the ancient idea that education pertains to a teacher sitting on a log with a student engaged in learning. California State University–San Marcos must meet the requirements for institutional accreditation as well as numerous other disciplinary-based accreditation standards. They must fill in numerous explanations to the state system about what they desire to do. As an institution, they need to develop job descriptions for the kinds of faculty positions they need. Promotion-and-tenure documents need to be written. The college catalogue and informational brochures must be developed. Student financial aid, registration, recruitment, and a retention plan must be put in place. Literally hundreds of such needs confront San Marcos administrators and faculty as they struggle to build a university.

And yet, because of these overwhelming demands, several fundamental issues do not seem to have been raised. There has not been any serious consideration about the relationship of pedagogy to the curriculum. Although many participants, for example, acknowledge that teaching is important and that prominence will be given to it in the promotion-and-tenure process, no one can define good teaching.

"The lecture seems to have gone out of fashion," commented one person, "and I'm not sure why." "I wish we were more informed about teaching; we will be once things calm down," said another. "I don't know what cooperative learning is. I've heard the name, that's all, and I've heard we should be doing it," said a third person. "It's immense what we need to do," explained another individual. Another person acknowledged how much needed to be done but also regretted that more attention had not been given to innovative issues:

We're becoming normal. We'll fit the mold, and I thought we would break the mold. Our teaching will be standard, and so will our curriculum. I understand why, of course, I'm not blaming anyone. The flood of work is unbelievable, but we could be different if we wanted to, there's still a chance here.

The one unique curricular innovation that San Marcos has developed is in terms of writing. Every class has a writing requirement of 2500 words. Regardless whether the course is English or computer science, history or physics, every student has to write at least 2500 words per course. The attitude toward the writing requirement seems mixed. "When it first started it was too tough," said a student. "Most of us have jobs or families, and to take a full load and expect ten-page papers in every class was too much." Another student continued, "But faculty have tried to accommodate us, so in some classes you'll keep a journal, or write smaller papers that add up to 2500 words in the semester."

Faculty also had reservations: "I'd never thought about writing before, and it was difficult at first." "They don't put the resources behind it that they should," said another. But in general faculty seemed pleased. One individual commented how it has made him concentrate on writing, for example, and another person pointed out "how it helps students communicate, and that's essential in today's world."

Yet again, like the view that the lecture is "out of fashion," the point here is not whether a writing requirement is a good or bad pedagogical tool, but that it has not been adopted as a philosophical statement about what constitutes excellent teaching and learning, and individuals do seem to need a sense of organizational philosophy. Some faculty see the writing requirement as helpful and others do not; some faculty have thought a lot about how they might creatively engage students with it and others see it as little more than something that needs to be done. And if resources are an indication of institutional commitment, then the writing requirement has received little commitment.

DIVERSITY AND DIFFERENCE

On Reinventing Education

Given the plethora of activities that need to be undertaken, one wonders how San Marcos would be different if administrators in the state system office had simply developed the policies and procedures rather than have faculty work on them as they now do. How would San Marcos differ if it had been set up on paper prior to anyone being hired? The answer is that it probably would not be very different from its current configuration. Colleges, the movement toward departments, requirements for the major, policies pertaining to promotion and tenure, and a host of other activities in which the institution is currently engaged all seem remarkably similar to what individuals in a state office might have envisioned.

Patrick Hill has pointed out that academe will remain oriented toward the status quo "if new voices and perspectives are added while the priorities and core of the organization remain unchanged" (1991, p. 45). To a certain extent, San Marcos is a good test case for Hill's assertion. The individuals who populate the academic roles are different from those of other institutions, but the structure has stayed relatively similar. At first glance, one wonders at the likelihood of moving toward a critical or postmodern perspective in a structure such as the one chosen at San Marcos; indeed, regardless of the perspective chosen, it seems that a concern about organizational structure is increasingly discussed by the initial participants themselves, who desired "something different, something new."

One significant difference, however, pertains not to the outcomes that are being generated but to the processes and socialization that are currently underway; that is, individuals are actively engaged in the construction of the institution. Presumably, such an engagement builds a particular ethos and camaraderie that would be absent if the individuals simply were hired and began their work as if they were at any other institution. "I came here to have a say in how things developed," said more than one person.

The manner in which one "has a say" ought to proceed and develop from a distinct educational philosophy that has yet to be articulated at San Marcos. An "education for the twenty-first century" is more than writing requirements and abstract statements about the values of good teaching. It also pertains to how decisions are made, to the kinds of goals established for curriculum and pedagogy, and, ultimately, what it means to be an educated citizen of the next century.

In large part, it appears that the structure imposed by the state and the fiscal depression in which California finds itself have overwhelmed the sense of agency that we might hope the organization's participants could exhibit. One possibility to deal with the dilemma of the state is to locate more consciously the problems, hopes, and visions of the institution in terms of institutional structure. To ensure that the institution reflects the desires of the members, individuals might more forcefully create a distinctive structure that is different from the multitude of other state colleges and universities. Rather than form around colleges and departments, the members might consider interdisciplinary units or centers, such as Science and Technology, or Cultural Studies. Instead of gradually moving toward a bifurcated decision-making apparatus of administration and faculty, the participants might make a conscious decision to keep decision making shared and communal. Promotion-and-tenure policies might be brought into question not in terms of what they "must" do to meet state requirements, but what could be done in terms of rewarding the community's members.

A mission statement that speaks distinctively to the clientele served might be developed rather than a mission document that is closer to what one participant at Huntsville described as "vanilla." The president had hoped that the mission of San Marcos would "engage people," but it appears that individuals have become so consumed with meeting the demands of different rules and procedures that they are being socialized not to the specific ideology of a particular institution, but to the unique needs of a new organization. The danger, of course, is that once the institution has passed its initial phase, the sense of organizational excitement that currently exists will die, and the lack of commonality that most individuals anticipate will occur. In a certain sense, it is as if individuals have become involved in a political campaign, and in the heat of the campaign, the excitement creates willpower and enthusiasm; yet ultimately, if a campaign is to succeed, it also generates unique ideas and hopes on the part of those involved.

I am concentrating on the problem of structure at San Marcos because it seems to have formed almost an organizational straightjacket that has made everyone there conform to the parameters of the state. To be sure, the manner in which dialogues occur and the ways individuals interact with one another are important. But at this point in the history of San Marcos, it seems that the way to create a sense of community and to build on the progress made by hiring to fulfill a design for diversity, necessitates bold initiatives that mark how the institution is different from, rather than similar to, other state universities. In this light, more forceful discussions about curricular, cocurricular and pedagogical alternatives seem warranted. My point here is obviously not to create something different simply for the sake of difference, but to engage consciously in the creation of an organizational structure that reflects the community's hopes and dreams rather than the state's plans.

Finally, as new faculty arrive at San Marcos, no formal socialization activities take place other than a series of informal meetings that highlight different tasks that need to be done. One may think it is presumptuous to deal with socialization when so much else needs to take place, but socialization occurs whether the institution plans explicit activities or not. "I just jumped in," said one individual about how he learned what to do. "You get on committees and you see everybody working hard. You get that sense when you interview," explained another person. Although both of these individuals could not point out any formal activities, socialization occurred through their observations of their colleagues and through the expectations placed on them. In large part, these expectations do not focus on intellectual discussions about the nature of pedagogy, for example, but instead involve building an academic major or participating on yet another search committee.

On Organizational Culture and Myth

Two interesting cultural artifacts of San Marcos are a photograph and a computer. The photograph, which is of the founding faculty and the president breaking ground for the new campus, is in many public places. The computer—found in virtually all offices—is a primary means through which individuals communicate with one another via electronic mail (e-mail). There is, then, a romanticized photograph that few institutions are able to exhibit in the same way; that is, most colleges and universities have such photographs or drawings, but they are reminiscent of the distant past, and myths about the individuals in the picture may exist, but no one knows them. The San Marcos photograph, however, is not simply a historical artifact; it is testimony to the present and the future. The photograph is also prominent in many of the founders' offices; indeed, the title found next to their names is "founding faculty," again highlighting how the institution is involved in the creation of its history.

As noted, San Marcos is at present quite small—both physically and in terms of organizational participants. The faculty is expected to double each year, and in the near future will move onto their permanent campus, but even then, only the originally planned first phase of campus construction will have been completed. Even though everyone is in close proximity to one another, the organization's participants rely heavily on communicating via e-mail. "It's efficient," said one person, and anyone who has used it could not argue the point. Yet e-mail also has other ramifications: "It's easier to get things said when it's impersonal," said one person. Another added, "I got home the other night and my phone messages told me to read my e-mail because of a flare out that had happened that day." A disagreement had occurred and individuals had responded by way of their computers.

Perhaps, in the postmodern world, telecommunications is the defining symbol of the way we interact with one another. CNN (Cable News Network) makes faraway worlds seem close; computer networks enable instant communication with one's colleagues three time zones away; conference calls with different parties on different continents have become commonplace. And yet, we still feel the need for myth and symbol in our lives. We point to photographs or signs or institutional histories not only as documents to our past but also as indications about the way we are to live with one another in the future.

The participants at San Marcos have struggled to meet the demands placed on them as they rush headlong into the twenty-first century. These demands and time constraints ought not to compromise a vision of the future that reaches out of America's democratic past. If postsecondary institutions in general have lost a sense of purpose or direction, then it falls upon newer institutions such as San Marcos to reinvent education and offer distinct possibilities that have been overlooked by more traditional colleges and universities. Indeed, the vast majority of the participants at San Marcos went there to do just that. It appears time for them to take a collective breath and define what they mean by a twenty-first century education even while they face the most difficult of fiscal times. Indeed, any of the individuals at the institutions discussed in chapters 4, 5, and 6, as well as the participants at the myriad other colleges and universities that account for postsecondary education in the United States, also need to consider how our education and organizations will be different in a century vastly different from the one we inhabit. We turn now to one possible interpretation of a reformulated education.

Chapter Seven

Cultural Citizenship and Educational Democracy

Postmodernism and critical theory share a concern for the re-searcher/author's position and the manner in which social science data is collected, analyzed, and presented. Unlike positivism and other related theories, critical theory and postmodernism assume that no privileged positions exist so that the role of the author—regardless of theoretical orientation—is inherently subjective. As Stuart Hall argues, "There's no enunciation without positionality. You have to position yourself *somewhere* in order to say anything at all" (1990, p. 18). Hall's comment highlights the stark contrast between theories that assume an essentialist role for the author, and projects such as postmodernism and critical theory that have as a core belief anti-essentialism.

Where postmodernism and critical theory have differed is in the nature of how and where one locates oneself. From a critical theory perspective, positioning oneself has meant to become actively engaged in reducing oppression in society. A postmodern critique has dealt with coming to terms with where one is situated in relation to issues such as race, class, gender, and sexual orientation. In other words, critical theory has been more concerned with the political nature of research, and postmodernism has focused on identity and difference and how to frame research questions, analyses, and answers. To be sure, one may infer that both theories inform one another: a concern with oppression inevitably involves breaking down hegemonic discourse; a focus on identity is inherently political. These connections have not always been seen as mutually compatible, however, and to some, they have seemed contradictory. In large part, one of the goals of this text has been to develop more explicitly the theoretical intersections of critical theory and postmodernism in order to create an alternative analysis of the problems and solutions that confront academe.

What remains are three tasks. First, I need to situate myself in this text more directly than I have. In doing so, I will discuss the method and design of this study and my own background and experiences that helped frame the undertaking. I will then return to a consideration of critical postmodernism and contrast it with three other views of the academy. I do so by suggesting how proponents of these views might interpret the data that has been presented. I will conclude by offering strategies for change. I will offer suggestions on two levels—that of the organization of academe, and that of the classroom.

THE ARCHITECTURE OF OUR LIVES

Parameters that Framed the Study

I will briefly outline here the method utilized to collect and analyze data in order to demonstrate the similarities and differences with previous research efforts. There are those critics who believe that research from an alternative framework is either so different from traditional research or so subjective that the researcher neither has any ties to traditional research nor to the development of any research design. From this perspective, critical ethnographers, for example, have been accused of sloppy, slipshod work that is merely used to prove their theoretical points. Criticism such as this fails to understand accurately the nature of qualitative research in general, and critical or postmodern work in particular. Obviously, as with any qualitative researcher, there are practical issues that I had to decide such as whether to tape-record or transcribe the interviews, which people to interview, and how to analyze the transcripts. Contradictory comments about similar events also had to be interpreted and understood.

All of these points are problems that any qualitative researcher has; the differences often result not so much in the methodological tools used, but in the manner in which the questions are framed, whose voices get heard, and how the findings are interpreted. For example, the research design I employed at Sherman College was relatively similar to what a functionalist might have used—a random sample of faculty, administrators, and students based on a number of variables such as age, gender, disciplinary background, and the like. The manner of interpretation will have differed, however, because of the theoretical orientation. Rather than look for similarities and assume that different opinions were a problem to be solved, I argued that someone's background and position in the organization afforded different interpretations.

The data for all of the chapters derive from case studies and interviews conducted between January 1991 and May 1992. The parameters of the investigation developed in light of the institution and my foci. Because of the size of Deep Springs College, for example, I was able to interview virtually everyone who was in attendance—faculty, students, staff, and the lone administrator. At Normal State University I only desired interviews with gay faculty to come to terms with the struggles they faced because of their sexual orientation. I entered San Marcos with the intent of examining the relationship between external influences and the organizational structure that developed at a new institution. In contrast, my goal at Huntsville College was to study the decision-making processes utilized by an institution to create a climate for change and innovation. Regardless of the differences in purpose between San Marcos and Huntsville, my interview format was the same. I interviewed a representative sample of faculty, administrators, and students. Obviously, because of the size of San Marcos, I was able to interview a greater percentage of the faculty and administration than at Huntsville, but Huntsville also enabled greater breadth and depth of interviews in particular areas, such as planning and analysis.

I interviewed close to 150 people for this study. Typically, the interviews ranged from sixty minutes to more than four hours. I utilized a life history format (Tierney, forthcoming b) for one of the interviews with a gay faculty member that was vastly more time-consuming than any other standard interview; it accounted for over thirty hours of taped conversation and several additional hours of note-taking. With the standard case studies at Sherman, Huntsville, and San Marcos, I called upon multiple interview strategies—one-on-one, couples, and small groups. One of the advantages of dual and small group interviews is that they allow individuals to play off of one another in a more dialogical format than one-on-one interviews typically allow. One of the difficulties of group interviews is the dynamics involved. Obviously, untenured faculty may be more reticent to discuss the problems they face when their department chairs are involved in the same interview. Faculty may hesitate to discuss the problems they have with the administration if the president is sitting in the room.

This project employed the most diverse methodological tools that I have heretofore attempted. Previously, I have used one method in the development of a text. In one study, for example, I conducted an ethnography (Tierney, 1988a), and in another work I utilized multiple case studies (1989). It seemed appropriate, however, to call upon diverse methodological strategies in a text that seeks to enable the reader to hear the multiple voices at work in academe. A standard case study would probably not have enabled gay faculty the space they needed to tell their story. Certainly a one-hour interview would not have adequately captured the struggles faced by an individual with AIDS in a hostile college environment. An ethnography would not have allowed for the breadth I desired to contrast the internal and external challenges that academic institutions face. And interviews without the complementary contextual site-specific data would have robbed the reader of understanding the intricacies of an institution such as Deep Springs.

Since critical postmodernism rejects distanced objectivism, it is also fair to ask how my ideas have changed during the course of this study. Indeed, critical postmodernism demands not only that I come to terms with how my ideas may have changed due to a particular investigation, but also how my actions have been informed by the inquiry. How has what I have learned led to action? To position myself, then, is not merely to locate my own biases of how I conducted a study, but I also must come to terms with my role vis-à-vis the struggles in the study. And these struggles are involved both with the people interviewed for the research and my actions on a daily level.

As noted at the outset, in some respects in calling for an understanding of how our theoretical formulations inform our practical existence, I am contradicting the ideas of multiple identities, as if one's theoretical self is separate from one's daily self. I write from singular and multiple identities. I am positioned by experiences and insights that give me a unique perspective with which to analyze a particular set of data; my theoretical and personal self are joined so that the public/private dichotomy is brought into question. By calling for research that incorporates singular and multiple perspectives, I am suggesting that we must investigate the standpoints from which we write, and we must acknowledge that our findings derive not merely from our theoretical formulations, but also from our private lives. Patricia Hill Collins, for example, has argued (1986) for black women to use as a strength their "outsider within" status in academe, where they utilize not only their formal academic training but also their experiences as black women.

In using multiple standpoints to critique data, we act in a manner akin to what Antonio Gramsci termed "organic intellectuals" (1971) or Henry Giroux has called "border intellectuals" (1992), by which we question traditional academic discourse from multiple perspectives. We do so not only by calling on our theoretical understanding of the world, but we also use our own backgrounds and subjectivities. And like our theoretical understanding of the world, our backgrounds are neither static nor determined. We are both subjects and objects in a world that constantly influences the way we interpret that world. Someone who is an African American woman in the academy uses her "outsider within" status not merely as if either the term *African American* or *woman* implies a fixed interpretation of a situation or context, but rather by recognizing that one's identity as an African American woman constantly undergoes change and transformation but that nevertheless gives a specific understanding of the world. And this understanding, as a border intellectual, is used to helped transform the world. Thus, I have used critical postmodernism as a theoretical construct to analyze the data, and I have tried to position myself in relation to the data. By decentering and personalizing the discourse, I run the standard risks of alternative research methodologies, and yet to absent myself from the text would defy the construct I have built.

Audre Lorde has spoken of poetry as the "architecture of our lives" (1984, p. 37). I have borrowed her term as a title for this section because it well suits the theory and methodology of critical postmodernism. Critical postmodernists are trying to fashion a discourse that re-presents the voices and experiences of people often on the margins.

As researchers/authors/intellectuals, we are conscious of how we have insinuated ourselves into the data, and we have the obligation to explain how we have functioned and how we will function, not simply as researchers or authors or intellectuals but as human beings. As Lorde comments, this architecture "lays the foundation for a future of change, a bridge across our fears of what has never been before" (1984, p. 37). How, then, do I interpret these case studies? How did what I found change my theoretical orientation, and how has it changed my action on a daily basis?

Theory/Praxis and the Role of the Public Intellectual

I already have alluded to changes in my thinking due to the interviews. Deep Springs College demonstrated that multiple ways exist for an education to be concerned with understanding the Other. San Marcos raised a question for me about the extent to which external ideas structure the outcome even before institutional actors come together to decide the purpose of their organization. Huntsville brought into question the utility of strategic planning, and Sherman forced me to concentrate on the nature of assessment. Prior to interviewing the gay faculty, and in particular the man with AIDS, I had not concentrated fully enough on the nature of academic community and how the problematic use of the word "community" excludes individuals. Conversely, I had neither gone to Deep Springs with the idea that I would find an education concerned with empowerment, nor had I assumed that the power of the state would be as great as it appears to be at San Marcos.

These ideas helped inform my thinking about critical postmodernism in several ways. The stories of gay faculty about their lives reinforced the need to blend critical theory and postmodernism insofar as an analysis of identity left me feeling that those individuals on the margins must be enabled to confront the oppression they face. A postmodern critique of identity that is void of action seems little more than the development of a taxonomy of difference for a postmodern mausoleum. Critical theory's lack of analysis of identity highlights that it has not fully come to grips with how we understand the silences that persons such as gay faculty feel they must keep.

Deep Springs underscored the inevitable tensions that exist between individuals and community; in studying a small college in the desert, I better understood postmodernism's emphasis on difference and critical theory's unending search for meaning. How do groups and individuals resolve differences and maintain their unique identities? What is the purpose of communal life? The responses that Deep Springers have developed to these questions helped frame my ideas about agape, hope, and the need for political action. Again, if I had only analyzed Deep Springs from a critical perspective, I may well have missed the interactions between individuals and the larger community; some versions of postmodernism would have overlooked the purpose of the community— its processes and purposes.

San Marcos enabled me to investigate culture and structure. On the one hand, I had to reformulate an idea previously developed about how culture operates in an organization; on the other hand, I was able to refine how the ideology of the state influences action. One of the underlying dilemmas for organizational participants that San Marcos brought out was how there does not seem to be time to develop an explicit educational philosophy, but in lieu of such discussions, one develops anyway.

What this research has done for me personally is to offer hints about local actions that I need to undertake as a faculty member and as a citizen of a university. Thus, the research has helped me redefine the role of a public intellectual in a postmodern world. Too often we have thought of praxis in a unitary fashion as if the only way one ought to conduct research and engage in praxis is to work with teachers to change the conditions the researcher found in the classroom. I do not question the importance of such action, but I offer here a variety of other actions that might be considered praxis-oriented. I offer these suggestions because they expand opportunities for action rather than restrict them to a specific site. I am also suggesting that an individual who considers himself or herself as a public intellectual must be involved in actions that involve praxis; theoretical argument by itself is a necessary but insufficient act.

For example, the problems of decision making and budget cutbacks discovered at Huntsville and San Marcos also have become concerns at my own institution; as these problems have grown, I have worked to create an oppositional voice, expressing more creatively and concretely what we intend for a philosophy of education. In doing so, I have called upon much of what I found at Deep Springs and critiqued at Sherman as a way to develop action.

I have testified before the legislature about student-oriented outcomes. My testimony has rejected standard formulas for outcomes such as I discussed for Sherman, and I explicitly situated the idea of assessment in terms of multiculturalism and diversity. I referred to the problems that gay people face. I argued that an education for excellence must include those individuals at the margins not simply as another group to be added into a melting pot, but as a way to reconceptualize how we think about academic communities.

I have worked assiduously on my own campus on issues of diversity and in particular about the problems that the gay faculty of Normal State voiced. By hearing the concerns of Normal State's faculty I have been able to develop more concretely in my teaching an explicit awareness of the multiple, changing identities we carry as students and faculty; I try constantly to be aware of how I am privileging and silencing individuals both in my teaching and in my role as an advisor. Deep Springs also helped me reflect on how to develop a course of study that more fully engages students in a self-reflective manner so that issues of identity, roles in reformulating education, and participation in democracy become central. The issue of socialization and, in particular, the problems faced by those of us who are different have encouraged me to plan a project that will study socialization and peer review.

I offer these points not to suggest that my work is in any way extraordinary, but rather as points that highlight action. Indeed, far too often we think of actors and actions as heroic and remarkable—Martin Luther King, Jr.'s speeches and marches come to mind. For those of us who do not have the sweeping vision or eloquence of a Dr. King, we are left feeling as if we have little to contribute to a movement for change. I am suggesting the opposite; there are countless actions in which each individual can participate in order to create a public arena where agape becomes the organizing concept and the conditions for hope are realized.

And our actions will be different from the norm. From a functional standpoint, numerous faculty testify before a congressional hearing or develop a research project out of a current study. Numerous other faculty eschew any action that involves practice or change-oriented work. Critical postmodernism demands action, but it is different from conservative or liberal acts that seek to reassert the primacy of norms.

The actions in which I have been engaged have been tied to the theoretical formulations considered early in this text. To be sure, I often have fallen short of my own hopes. I also do not discount the privileged status I inhabit as a tenured faculty member at a research university. Presumably, the writing of this text enhances my own career and does nothing for an individual interviewed for the study, although I point out that, as a small step towards change, half of the royalties for this book will be donated for AIDS research.

Commonsensically, I know I cannot escape who I am, but critical postmodernism has taught me to understand the fissures of identity and to try to make connections so that I am more than merely a unitary author creating an objective text. I am also a teacher who is forced to reflect on his own pedagogic strengths and weaknesses when confronted with an educational community in the desert. I am a policy analyst who responds to issues of assessment, a faculty voice working on numerous faculty committees, and a gay man who has seen too many friends and colleagues die of AIDS. All of these selves unite in text. As the author, I have an obligation not simply to develop a research design and present data in as careful a manner as possible, but also to develop strategies in my own life that will change the oppressive aspects that I have found in the various arenas of the research effort. Thus, I not only try to report accurately on the architecture of our academic lives, but I also try to become an architect myself and enable others to do so as well as we create "the foundations for a future of change." I turn now to one of the fundamental foundations of this text.

RETHINKING CULTURE

We have arrived at a point in time where many of our most pressing concerns ultimately turn on how we define culture, and relatedly, ideology. In large part, the conservative critique of academe that arose during the Reagan era was not merely over whether to teach one author or another, but rather, how to configure what we mean by an academic institution. I offer the four primary views of culture and how they relate to the way we think about and act in colleges and universities. In doing so, I call upon the theoretical notions developed in Chapters 1, 2, and 3 and the data from the case studies to highlight the radically different conceptions.

Academe as a Cultural Museum

This view of culture has attracted the most attention and is the least representative of those individuals involved in academe. Arguments have taken place over the canon, and the assumption has been that a set body of literature needs to be transmitted to our youth so that they will be able to learn the traditions and truths that have been handed down generation to generation.

The chief proponents of this view have been Allan Bloom (1987), Dinesh D'Souza (1991), and Roger Kimball (1990). Their books were published in mainstream presses, received widespread recognition, and were written in a prose accessible to those outside of academe. The tenor of the argument has often been apocalyptic and has created a relationship between what its proponents perceive as the lowering of academic standards and the decline of Western civilization. "Their [e.g., postmodernists, feminists, decontructionists] object," states Kimball, "is nothing less than the destruction of the values, methods, and goals of traditional humanistic study" (1990, p. xi). "An academic and cultural revolution is under way at American universities," continues D'Souza (1991, p. 13). "The university has become inundated and saturated with the backflow of society's problems," writes Saul Bellow in Bloom's text (1987, p. 12).

The implications of the conservative critique are multiple. The curriculum is perceived as the content of what is taught in a class, and the content is judged as masterpieces that have been determined by experts and the test of time. Those who teach the masterpieces should be the most qualified individuals in their respective fields as determined by objective criteria such as examinations. Students should have entrance requirements, constant evaluations, and final examinations that will gauge how much they have learned. Such assessment measures will be able to test not only the student, but also the teacher and institution as well.

There is a curious sense of engagement and disengagement with the "real world" held by proponents of this position. In its purest form, the conservative argument paints the academy in its historic position as a group of intellectuals removed from the affairs of everyday life in order to do battle over life's great truths. At the same time, the conservatives point out that university life is one of the central causes of societal problems. The portrait enables conservatives to decry the "politicization" of the academy in one breath and in the next describe how such political tactics have created the moral decay of society. Such a view is consistent if we hold to a traditional definition of knowledge. In this light, colleges are museums that point out what is best in society. The decline of societal concern about the upkeep of the museum points to the decline of societal values. The lack of values destroys America's work ethic, which, in turn, makes America less competitive in the marketplace.

The conservatives desire to change the academy generally by turning back many of the "assaults" that they perceive to have taken place. D'Souza offers the clearest proposals. *Affirmative action* based on race should be dropped; race- or gender-based admissions or hiring criteria should be foresworn. Indeed, any congregating on campus due to categories such as race, gender, or sexual orientation should be prohibited; D'Souza, for example, states his model university "would not permit a Black Students Association" (1991, p. 253). Although the study of other cultures may by a viable option, the core of study should be "familiarity with the founding principles of one's own culture" (1991, p. 255). Diversity is defined in terms of philosophic diversity and has little, if anything, to do with issues of race, class, or gender; Western civilization is defined as "one's own culture."

In general, the portrait of academe drawn here is a desire for a return to institutions that once populated America's landscape but that, in many respects, no longer represent American higher education. Most of the discussion that takes place in conservative circles focuses on traditionally aged students who attend elite institutions such as Stanford, Dartmouth, or Chicago. The problems that community colleges face or that adult students encounter are generally forgotten. Most of the criticism of faculty derives from academic celebrities such as Stanley Fish of Duke University or the French deconstructionist Jacques Derrida. The concerns raised by lesbian and gay students, or, in particular, by women, are brushed aside as irrelevant and politically motivated. The mundane, day-to-day problems dealt with by Huntsville's or Sherman's faculty are never considered.

As with any school of thought, the conservative critique is not monolithic. D'Souza and Kimball and Bloom undoubtedly differ with one another, but their similarities are greater than their differences. The conservatives would have interpreted the case studies for this book in very different fashion from the manner in which I have. Although Deep Springs, for example, in some respects reflects an institution where learning takes place in ways the conservatives admire, surely the way in which I have defined education for empowerment would seem absurd. From a conservative standpoint, an education concerned with understanding the Other takes a distant second place to an approach investigating the classics. Further, the idea that students are capable of hiring faculty or choosing the curriculum is ludicrous. The thought that education has anything to do with working on a ranch, or that a rancher is a teacher, is ridiculous to individuals who subscribe to the conservative agenda.

And, of course, the concerns of gay faculty have nothing to do with an academic institution. At the worst, such faculty have an immoral agenda they wish to foist on the academy; at the very least, the personal lives of academics should not be a point of investigation. A classroom, and by extension a college, is about the life of the mind. It is a public arena in which individuals argue about ideas. What an individual does in the privacy of his or her home should be kept private. To make public what is private detracts from the central issues of a classroom and brings into question "real world" concerns that should otherwise be left at academe's door. From this perspective, the focus of the academy is on the search for "Truth," and it can only be done in the rarefied atmosphere of a classical college.

Consequently, the issues raised in Sherman or Huntsville lose their importance. Perhaps the best that can be said is that faculty should leave governance to presidents and their administrations. To be sure, assessment is important, but not because it has anything to do with "organizational culture"; assessment is significant so that what students learn can be measured. Such measurement can be done relatively easily if there is agreement about what is to be taught. Similarly, the philosophic diversity of San Marcos might be looked on by the conservatives with pleasure, but the concern for gender and racial diversity that San Marcos has placed at the top of its agenda is only more evidence of the politicization of the academy. In this light, San Marcos students are being shortchanged a quality education because hiring committees are not looking for the best teachers but instead are trying to find "female teachers" or "African American teachers."

And if the conservatives might express displeasure with what they would find at these institutions, they would be equally upset with the conclusions that I have offered. The idea that pedagogy ought to be linked to the curriculum, that we should decenter norms or develop an ideal of democracy that is related to structure and ideology are precisely the kinds of recommendations that the conservatives decry. The ideal of the academy as a museum where the participants neutrally view the cultural artifacts of the past stands in sharp contrast to an ideal of the academy as a place where public intellectuals need to be engaged with the life of society, and where teaching and learning cannot be divorced from those whom we taught in the classroom.

Perhaps because of the eloquence and stridency of their language, the conservatives have garnered the most notice, but the fewest advocates. Although individuals may agree with parts of their arguments, few people believe that the academy should be divorced from the everyday concerns of common citizens. And these common citizens are people of all colors, of both genders, of varying sexual orientation, and a host of other diverse constituencies. A parallel in the "real world" to the Blooms and Kimballs of the academic world might be found in Randall Terry's Operation Rescue, which seeks to close women's health clinics that offer abortions. The extremism of his position has guaranteed him media attention. Although some individuals may agree with some part of his argument, opinion polls continually point out society's widespread disdain for the terrorist tactics Terry uses. The same might be said for the apocalyptic version of the academy that the conservatives seek to promulgate with their "scorched earth" rhetoric.

Academe as a Cultural Stew

The most widely held opinion of academe is one that has ties to the cultural museum, but gives credence to diversity and multiculturalism. This is a view that originates in a liberal humanist ideology that aims to promote cultural homogeneity. From this perspective, problems such as racism or sexism are problems with which academe should be concerned, but these problems are essentially surface-level problems rather than structural issues. The solution to race-related issues is to change people's minds and to enable more faculty and students of color to enter academe. A more inclusive curriculum is necessitated, and faculty have an obligation to understand the diversity that exists within their classrooms.

Interestingly, liberal humanists may interpret the data presented here in a manner akin to what I have done, but they will disagree with my conclusions. Again, liberal humanists do not speak with one voice, but their ideas derive from the same cloth. Consequently, they might well agree with the problems that gay faculty face, and they will find much to admire in Deep Springs. They will understand the problems encountered at Sherman with regard to the lack of community, and they will applaud the hiring by design for diversity at San Marcos. Indeed, a functional analysis of San Marcos has also highlighted the sense of disenchantment faculty feel at the institution (Gorman, 1992, p. B3).

The difference between liberal humanism and critical postmodernism surfaces most clearly if we return to the discussion in Chapters 1, 2, and 3 and the subsequent analyses I have offered of the case studies. The cultural view of academe as a stew, or melting pot, operates on a consensus model. Differences are looked on as attributes, but they do not necessitate structural changes. We train people—women, blacks—to fit into the norms that are established. This is the view I discussed in the first chapter, which says that some people have culture and others are devoid of it; we know who are "different" because they are not similar to "us." The vision of community, then, is framed around multiple voices that speak the same language rather than voices that speak across sharp differences. Essentially, the idea of the academy as a cultural stew avoids discussion of power and structure. Giroux offers a helpful contrast between critical postmodernism and liberal humanism:

Those designated as Others need to both reclaim and remake their histories, voices, and visions as part of a wider struggle to change those material and social relations that deny radical pluralism as the basis of democratic political community. . . . It is not enough for students to learn how to resist power which is oppressive, and prevents them from struggling against forms of power that subjugate and exploit (1990, p. 29).

Giroux highlights how the liberal humanist does not so much dispute as ignore many of the ideas linked with critical postmodernism. The concept of difference or the idea that individuals simultaneously hold multiple identities is not mentioned. The thought that oppression is a structural problem that demands solutions that decenter norms and recreate boundaries and border zones is overlooked. How power operates as a force for oppression and might be configured as a source of resistance is avoided. To be sure, the idea of hope exists, but it is not so much an idea of hope whereby communities work out their differences through ongoing dialogues of respect. Instead, hope is the idea of a future Utopia that can be achieved; in this Utopia everyone lives in harmony and agreement. The role of the academic is not to be involved in political action, but rather to involve himself or herself in studies that advance our understanding of truth.

With the liberal humanist ideal, we have, then, a curious blending of the conservative and the critical postmodern critique. From this perspective, we recognize the importance of including different people within the academy and the concomitant changes that this will entail such as within the curriculum or in hiring practices. Nevertheless, the modernist ideal remains intact. Consensus is achievable. A community functions around norms. Ultimate truths exist.

This view is by far the norm in academe. And as a norm, it asks the least of individuals and of the institution. If we do not think that sexism is a structural problem or that, in turn, ideology and culture frame sexism, then we neither need to change our own actions or those of the institution. We are able to create minor changes and to expect that once we have allowed a different group entrance to the academy then everything else will follow. I suggest that this is the norm in academe because the vast majority of those of us who populate higher education have a desire to keep invisible norms in place. We agree to the creation of a women's studies department if it conforms to common conceptions of what we think of as knowledge and of a department. We hire a minority affairs coordinator so that someone is able to deal with a particular group rather than assume that the task belongs to everyone.

In contrast, critical postmodernism demands structural change that begins with individuals' awareness of their biases and limitations. The problem turns not on new members conforming to the institution, but to the institution trying to create conditions by which we honor difference. We constantly make visible the norms of the institution and question them so that newer members do not simply become socialized to these norms, but rather, individuals in the community try to come to terms with the differences of others. Community is in constant negotiation, dialogue, and reformulation.

Cultural Separatism and the Academy

With its roots in postmodernism, cultural separatism subscribes to the idea that different groups have distinct identities and the differences are so great that one group has little, if anything, to share in common with another. Like those who advocate the museum school of culture, this group is equally small, but their vision is so clear that they often are the easiest to attack. The idea of separatist aesthetics and politics is one that is lodged in areas that seek to build in-group solidarity and destroy norms that are seen as privileged toward male, heterosexual, Eurocentric thought.

Although the ideas offered from this perspective are often abstract and academic, they also lend themselves easily to unfair caricature and ridicule. Images of men being tossed out of women's studies classes, of whites not allowed entrance to black studies courses, of "homosexuals" with an "agenda," are replete in books such as those written by the cultural conservatives. In contrast, cultural separatists focus on the symbols and communicative vehicles of the academy to point out how different groups are relegated to the border zones of the academy.

Cultural separatists would critique San Marcos as an institution that has fallen into the trap of simply mirroring the power of the norm. They would recognize the problems that the gay faculty face but might question the manner in which these faculty are portrayed—as weak and silenced, rather than as strong and vocal. They might argue that such portraits only reaffirm the idea of a group on the fringes, rather than projecting a vision of separatist political groups, which groups such as Queer Nation espouse. Similarly, the idea that Deep Springs could become involved in a discussion of the Other in the very absence of those who are different would be rejected, and the argument that a comparative awareness might enable faculty to understand the organization of other campus cultures would be seen as irrelevant, if not a way to obscure the structural changes that need to take place.

From the position developed here, the problem of a vision of culture as separatist is that it denies the possibility for human agency, hope, or agape. Individual constraints are seen as so overwhelming as to deny any chance of pluralist action. Although there is much to learn from the separatist critique, ironically, often it ends up in the position that it challenges. The argument that my position is unique and so different that no one else can possibly understand it or speak with me denies voice to everyone but myself. Obviously a heterosexual cannot understand what it means to be gay, lesbian, or bisexual. A Caucasian cannot know what it means to be a Native American. Once we understand this point, however, the question turns on what we do then. The cultural separatist often appears to mirror the idea that since I cannot understand your reality I am absolved of further action, and I am denied the voice of solidarity. Critical postmodernists offer a different analysis, which I turn to now.

Cultural Citizenship in the Academic Community

Here we have a view of culture as contested terrain that involves a politics of difference and coalition-building. The idea of *cultural citizenship* extends beyond geographic boundaries as if we are only citizens in nation-states. Instead, cultural citizenship involves transcending borders and trying to understand cultural difference. We honor one another's identities not by assuming we can amalgamate differences, but by engaging in dialogues of respect and understanding. Because of the abstraction of this argument, we run the risk either of creating a misunderstanding on the part of individuals or of denying them the possibility of constructing actions for their own lives. How do we transcend borders? How do we come to understand cultural difference? I do not have specific instructions to follow, but there is a schema that might be considered.

Some years ago I worked at a Native American community college. As one of the few white people at the institution, I found myself in the position of being a racial minority. Years before that as a Peace Corps volunteer, I had lived in a Berber town in the Atlas mountains of northwest Africa where I was the only non-Moroccan. I worked my way through college working in a homeless shelter in inner-city Boston. As a gay man, I have constantly been in positions where no one else who works with me is openly gay. Obviously, I am neither suggesting that everyone needs to travel to the Magrib to understand the Other, nor that simply by living with people different from ourselves do we honor difference. In fact, the colonial mentality is most often evident when different groups come in contact with one another. The French colonial racism in Morocco, the white landowners' economic stranglehold on American Indian reservations, and the genocidal attacks of the Serbian majority on the Bosnians are painful examples of the failure of what I have called cultural citizenship.

If we agree on the idea of agape and the concept of fundamental connection, however, then it is necessary to try to understand others' realities, and we do this in a manner akin to what I have suggested here. We come to understand one another not by broad, sweeping actions, but by living and learning on a daily basis. We are not tourists on a week-long excursion with a guidebook in our hands to show us the interesting sites and lives of a people. To the contrary, we cannot understand differences in a momentary, fragmentary fashion, and we do not have a Michelin guide to tell us what to do.

Instead, we engage people where we are most at risk with questioning our own identities, and we do so through prolonged involvement. By use of the word "we," I mean all people. No one holds a privileged knowledge of cross-cultural communication, as if simply because I am gay I will somehow understand the experiences of Asian Americans or the physically challenged. By "risk," I mean that we need to do more than simply see the film *Dances with Wolves* and assume we understand the Native American condition, or give a donation to an AIDS project and think we have absolved our responsibility to people with AIDS. By "prolonged involvement," I mean that learning about the Other never stops; we are always in a process of redefinition.

For the academy, the implications of this view of culture are vast. As with the conservative critique that calls for sweeping change, if we subscribe to the idea of cultural citizenship as a model of connectedness and relatedness that revolves around honoring difference, then we are not merely suggesting that the curriculum needs to change. We define the idea of curriculum and knowledge as essentially a process that involves the construction and reformulation of identities of those individuals involved in the interaction. The teacher is less of an authority and more of an equal. Assessment lessens in importance, and the processes involved in the construction of the community become essential. Administrators are less involved in managing the enterprise and instead approach their work more as an intellectual task.

Thus, academe as a community revolves around interactional meanings and redefinitions of what it means to be a citizen. Such discussions neither happen simply on Friday afternoons in the president's office when there is an "open door," nor do they occur at the end of the semester when a faculty member has students over for a potluck. Instead, conversations of respect must reveal, as Estela Bensimon notes, "the values, beliefs, and views of reality that inform our thinking; we must make ourselves vulnerable" (1992, p. 2). The assumption here is that in a world where reality is constructed, and individuals have different interpretations of the world, the work of the community necessarily begins and continues with the idea that no one holds "true" understanding. Cultural citizenship, then, is an ongoing process that has as its focus the identity-work that postmodernism has highlighted, and the desire for democratic community that critical theory has underscored.

By "identity-work," I am suggesting that individuals come to understand their own and others' lives through prolonged engagement with the other. Rather than assume that one's indentity is fixed and determined, we are constantly in the process of redefinition and discovery.

The democratic community revolves around contradictions. We search for commonalities while encouraging difference. We seek community through conflict. We act as leaders by following. We develop voice by listening. We learn about ourselves by trying to understand others. We develop goals by concentrating on processes. We teach about norms while we encourage new members to change them. Each act in itself is not a magic potion to radically transform academic culture, but it offers a schema for thinking about higher education in a way radically different from ideas of colleges and universities as museums or "stews" or isolated arenas with unbridgeable differences. In the next section, I will expand on how we might create educational democracy in our institutions and classrooms, and attend to the initial questions raised in Chapter 1.

THE POLITICS OF DIFFERENCE

I am responding here with twelve propositions that point us in the direction of creating communities of difference: the first two set the thematic grounds for the remaining ten; of the remainder, five concern organizational strategies we might employ to create change, and five pertain to suggestions about how to reorient the classroom environment. The guiding question here is: If we assume a critical postmodern stance, what strategies might we develop to wrestle with the problems that confront academe? How do we create a climate where agape and hope are organizational and classroom processes and goals?

Develop Cultural Learning

As with any text, the possibility for misinterpreting what I have meant always exists. With regard to creating a climate for organizational change and agape, one of the central propositions that I need to clarify pertains to how citizens of a community become and remain border intellectuals. As Giroux notes, "Becoming a border crosser engaged in a productive dialogue with others means producing a space in which those dominant social relations, ideologies and practices that erase the specificity of the voice of the other must be challenged and overcome" (in press). Giroux's point refers to what I define as "cultural learning." How do we engage in practices that enable us to understand the Other?

A white college president who introduces an African American keynote speaker on Martin Luther King, Jr. Day may mistakenly feel that such activity is what I have called cultural learning. Similarly, a male college dean who is quick to point out that he is pro-choice, or a heterosexual provost who makes it known that she disagrees with the military's ban on gays, also may interpret such support as cultural learning. Obviously, activities that are the opposite of these examples are not what I desire. A president who consciously skips a multiracial activity or an administrator who neither cares about women's reproductive rights nor gay rights has moved away from the creation of a community of difference.

As we approach the twenty-first century, however, simply attending an event to signal our support is no longer sufficient. I define *cultural learning* as the development of, and engagement in, dialogues of support and understanding across differences. The geography, temporality, and discourse of these dialogues are powerful signals about one's desire to engage in cultural learning. We do not need to be a semiotician to understand the politics of space and time. When I enter a president's office, I am in the president's sphere; when the president enters a dormitory, she is on different turf. When the dean asks to see me at two o'clock on a Friday afternoon, I am fitting into his schedule; when the dean attends an evening fund-raiser for an AIDS project, he is meeting someone's else's time schedule. The first step in cultural learning, then, is the ability of an individual to step out of his or her geographic and temporal spheres of influence and into the spheres of others. Such a step is more complex than it appears, for in doing so, the learner is consciously giving up components of a strategy of power in order to learn about the Other.

The next step pertains to the individual's desire and ability to listen. A president who attends a secretarial meeting and spends 80 percent of the meeting talking about the problems of the institution is different from a president who comes to a meeting with a desire to understand the problems of a particular group. A faculty member who hears the problems of a lesbian student and begins to read books about lesbian and gay individuals is different from the professor who automatically sends the student to the counseling center for her "problems." A residence hall advisor who tries to learn sign language because one of the students on the floor is hearing-impaired is different from someone who simply tries to help the individual adapt.

Here, then, a person leads by following. We listen to what individuals have to say rather than fill the discursive space with our own voices. This form of listening is neither mindless acquiescence nor psychological analysis. We do not listen because our role demands that we attend one or the other meeting, and we do not listen to solve someone's problem. Far too often these are the forms of listening that we engage in with our students and colleagues. Instead, I am suggesting a listening that involves risk and courage. We listen to individuals' stories so that we might understand their views of the world, and in doing so, we may have to radically transform our own understandings.

The next step in cultural learning is the internalization of the Other's needs, wants, and desires. Again, the point is not to accept mindlessly what someone says, but to understand different people's views of the world so well that we incorporate these views in our own outlook. Cross-cultural awareness implies that the learner sustains relationships across differences and works to create an environment in which these differences are able to be voiced and heard. The cultural learner, then, does not speak for others, but works so that they, too, can speak.

Parenthetically, this point is difficult for an institution such as Deep Springs to enact, for even though Deep Springs students engage in dialogues about difference, the lack of racial and gender difference in the student body obviously does not allow for mutual dialogues.

To engage in cultural learning is hard, sustained work. Too often we want instant answers to difficult problems, when in fact the only way we can create meaningful answers involves making the time and effort to understand quite often remarkably different realities. Difference is confusing and threatening because we are forced to confront ideas and lives that often bring into question our own commonly held assumptions and beliefs. If we are unable to participate in dialogues that question our views of the world, then we have not been engaged in cultural learning.

Essentially, I am bringing into question the parameters of power we hold as individuals, so that we are more able to understand the concerns of people radically different from ourselves. I often have visited colleges and universities, for example, with a significant Native American student population, but a majority of the Caucasian administrators and faculty have never taken the time to visit an Indian reservation and learn about the ways of the tribe. I have heard administrators and faculty also relate that they do not know anyone who is gay or lesbian, unaware that they have peers and colleagues who are gay and lesbian but who are afraid to "come out" and reveal themselves. I have seen faculty skip workshops on sexism because they are "a waste of time," yet I have heard women students of these professors complain about the conditions in their classrooms.

The point is not that someone is a "bad" person, but that if we want to create the conditions for building a community of difference, then we must place at a premium an emphasis on creating cultural learners. How is it possible to honor difference if I have not made any effort to understand the backgrounds of my students? How can I be an effective department chair if I have never tried to understand a colleague who is gay? As a dean, how can I exemplify care for everyone in my college if I have not ensured that every possible effort has been made to make my building accessible to those in wheelchairs? If leadership is in some form defined by example, as a college president how can I argue that diversity is important if I do not learn about the manifold cultures of my institution?

Encourage Dangerous Memory

Cultural learning pertains to what an individual can do to understand other people's realities. Encouraging "dangerous memory" involves creating conditions so that the Other is able to speak from his or her personal and intellectual experience. "Dangerous memories," to use Sharon Welch's (1990) term, are those stories and experiences that have been silenced by the power of the norm discussed in Chapter 3. The purpose in telling these stories is not to find one true narrative tale to which we may all subscribe, but rather, as Sharon Welch points out, to "call upon those of us who are, often unknowingly, complicit in structures of control to join in resistance and transformation" (1990, p. 139).

When we enable others to speak from their personal experiences, we bring into question organizational norms and values and open up the possibility for significant changes in how we interact with one another. Memories that have been silent or subjugated are "dangerous" because developing voice inevitably involves issues of power. When people gain voice, they speak, and when they speak, the organization will have to respond. It is far easier to control a group if we assume that we all speak with one voice. If an institution seeks to homogenize its citizenry, then a black studies center, a commission for women, or a gay student union serves no purpose; I am suggesting that spheres of interest such as these serve a distinctly different purpose. When marginalized groups are able to come together and discuss each other's problems, hopes, and ideas, they are enabling dialogues built on collective memories that serve in the creation of communities of difference.

When a residence hall coordinator develops a cultural studies program for the dorm based on life histories of the students, she is engaged in the work of developing dangerous memories. When distinctly different groups such as returning adult students, the physically challenged, and Native Americans are all put into a multicultural resource center in order to "mainstream" and save funds, we are involved in the subjugation of dangerous memory. When a president says the college does not have the funds necessary to create a women's studies major, the decision is more than merely fiscal; the decision also has implications for the creation of sites and stories of resistance. When the board of trustees commissions a study about the problems that lesbian and gay individuals face at the institution, the institution becomes involved in encouraging dangerous memory. When a dean decides not to create a minor in gender education because it would not help students in the job market, then we discover the stifling of memories of difference and diversity.

With examples such as these, I run the risk of painting decision making as simpleminded, either-or choices. Either we create a gender education minor, or we do not. Either we visit an Indian reservation or we do not. The point, however, is not to suggest that gross dichotomies exist as if every institution is a photocopy of every other, but rather, to raise questions pertaining to the creation of communities of difference. If we truly want to engage in the work of critical postmodernism, then of necessity we must create a politics of difference that places every institutional member in a new location with regard to cultural identity. We break essentialist frames of thought, discourse, and action, and we seek conversations across differences. We accentuate difference rather than ameliorate it.

Cultural learning and dangerous memory are two themes that cut across organizational and classroom activities. They speak to a community that seeks cultural citizenship and a democratic pluralism. Like any beliefs, the road to action is neither uniform nor obvious. That is, because I have outlined a critical postmodern framework does not mean that I can now develop five simple steps that all administrators need to follow for organizational success. Huntsville's dilemmas are unique to Huntsville. At the same time, there are some actions that clearly do not lead to organizational agape. An organization that fires someone for no other reason than that he is gay or that refuses to hire a president because she is Hispanic, obviously acts against the grain of what I have developed here. A dean who does not solicit input or a student affairs vice president who refuses to meet with students who have a grievance is similarly acting in a manner distinctly different from the ideas of critical postmodernism. In what follows, I first offer five organizational ideas and then five ideas for the classroom that enhance cultural learning and dangerous memory. These themes derive from the case studies and the framework developed in the first three chapters, and much like the research methodology employed, they also are related to other strains of thought.

Organizations

Create a Framework for Diversity. I pointed out earlier how Deep Springs has struggled to understand the Other in the absence of "Others." San Marcos, on the other hand, has consciously hired people to insure that people of color and women are represented. The point here is that it is inconceivable to be a diverse institution if diversity is not a central concern. San Marcos and Deep Springs offer helpful examples of how academe ought to respond if it desires a community of difference.

I am fully cognizant that if every institution in America placed diversity at the top of its priorities, there would not be enough faculty of color to be hired. I am equally aware that, in certain disciplines such as engineering and physics, there are few women or people of color. But more often than not, I find such facts used as excuses by a department that says it cannot find a candidate. In an institution that places diversity as its highest priority, creative ways will be developed to enhance academic areas in order to attract diverse candidates. The first step is the creation of a plan for diversity.

An institution that desires diverse constituencies interacting with one another needs to create an agenda around which such dialogues can take place. Simply stated, when a college or university embarks on a fund-raising campaign, it has goals and objectives that are constantly monitored and evaluated; most often, the same cannot be said for an institution's plans for diversity. An institution needs to create an agenda with identifiable objectives and goals that highlight its plan to achieve multiculturalism in terms of those who teach, work, and study in the organization.

Once such an agenda is developed, the institution then needs to turn to an explicit analysis of how it intends to encourage, acculturate, and accommodate its new members. I pointed out with San Marcos that socialization occurs whether by design or by inference. At Sherman we saw similar learning occur where individuals struggled to define institutional purpose and, in its absence, sought meaning at the departmental level.

We also know that more faculty and students of color depart from an institution than do their white counterparts, and more women faculty and students also leave. In part, these departures occur because of the lack of communal structures that seek to create fellowship. Sherman College is an example of an institution moving toward defining the culture of its community. I am suggesting that an institution concerned about diversity will embark on such definitions in order to develop a concrete agenda about how it will function as a community of difference.

Initiate Structures for Developing Voice. The concerns of groups such as gay and lesbian faculty will go unheard unless an institution creates a structure for hearing the problems and concentrating on solutions. In a climate of fear and silence, an organization's participants do not discover incidents of sexual harassment or the problems of faculty of color unless they are investigated. Far too often institutions hesitate to study a problem because they do not want to uncover "bad news," which often refers to diversity-related issues.

In order to develop a more proactive stance to problems, institutions are well advised to incorporate into their structure ways to promote multiculturalism. Strategies might range from the creation of a specific individual in the president's office whose concern is diversity, to the creation of standing committees that offer recommendations and monitor progress. I am not suggesting that we isolate multicultural issues to one individual or a particular area; however, if an individual feels discriminated against or silenced and has no one in the institution who can deal with the concern, then we have a structural problem that needs to be remedied.

Similarly, when we look at a library and find that librarians are assigned for one form of scholarship but not another, we see the privileging of one area of study over another. When we discover that a student affairs office has a broad array of officers but no one whose concern is with the physically challenged, we find that a group is structurally invisible. In an institution that desires diverse curricula, the structure of the library will be used to accommodate diverse viewpoints such as feminist perspectives or Native American literature. A college that honors difference will use its structure to ensure that different constituencies are represented and served. Again, to suggest that structures change to incorporate diversity does not imply the quarantining of a particular people's concerns; rather, the suggestion highlights how the institution has developed a structural, sustained response to diversity rather than an ad hoc, reactive one.

Structures that develop voice are not merely related to decision making and governance. An institution that honors diversity will create arenas for diverse intellectual viewpoints to be brought forward and considered. Such arenas range from workshops and seminars initiated for the entire institution or its various constituencies, to small reading groups or presentations intended for a specific group such as a departmental faculty or a student affairs staff. If the topics for these structures are intellectually challenging and the institution embraces the ideas of agape, then significant individuals such as a president or dean will attend not because their presence is warranted, but because they have a genuine desire to learn. In so doing, cultural learning takes place, and the possibility for dangerous memory occurs.

Implement Alternative Structures of Learning. In the difficult times in which higher education now finds itself, we often discover commonalities across institutions in their responses to fiscal shortfalls. Fewer classes are offered. Class size increases. The fight over dollars creates greater competition across departments. The impulse is to mainstream different groups. The suggestion here is to think in a different manner about teaching and learning. An institution that as a central core of its ideology forms a commitment to critical pedagogy and the development of border intellectuals will have a curricular structure quite different from that of the panoply of institutions that currently exist in the United States.

We learned from Deep Springs how everyone in the institution can be engaged in democratic discourse. If we translate that lesson to other institutions, then it seems imperative that, at a minimum, every individual will be involved in some form of a learning community. Such a suggestion implies that all administrators will return to the classroom every year and teach a class, that the most powerful faculty—those who inhabit endowed chairs and distinguished professorships—will be centrally engaged in undergraduate teaching and learning, and that the sharp distinctions that now exist between teaching faculty and research faculty will be lessened. Further, staff will be encouraged to get involved in the learning process, and students will be given every option to be more involved as colearners rather than as passive participants.

The creation of alternative structures of learning also suggests that the stranglehold that departments currently have on resources, faculty appointments, and the creation of curricula needs to change. At the least, we need to develop arenas in which proponents of diverse viewpoints can come together around common themes and ideas in intellectual dialogue that often cannot occur in a department that anoints one discourse as supreme. I am suggesting that centers for interdisciplinary study and institutes for cross-cultural teaching and learning offer necessary bases for cultural learning and dangerous memory that often cannot take place in existing departments.

Develop Assessment as a Formative Activity. Deep Springs and Sherman College offered a helpful counterpoint for discussing assessment. Rather than develop external and summative criteria, I have suggested that we create assessment as an ongoing process that involves the entire community. Such an activity both involves cultural learning and dangerous memory insofar as we request all individuals to confront one another over the tasks in which they are engaged.

Far too often only one's superiors participate in evaluation. A unit head evaluates the unit. The department evaluates the untenured professor. The professor evaluates the class. Rather than creating hierarchical models for evaluation, an organization concerned with agape focuses on processes and teamwork in the development of assessment measures. A team approach to assessment offers one danger and multiple advantages. The danger of a team is that it can move toward groupthink that excludes individuals and different ideas (Bensimon & Neumann, 1993). Once we are aware of such dangers, however, we are able to create the conditions by which disagreement, rather than agreement, forms the framework for the team.

The advantages of a team approach to assessment pertain to the discussion about the relationship to an individual's work in a community. If we desire democratic participation in our activities, we need to enable all individuals to engage in the governance of the institution. On an individual level, this implies that a department needs to structure times when the group evaluates and discusses the work of the unit and when the individuals speak with one another about their interactions. On a broader level, this means that participation is valued because the work of the community could not continue without everyone's input. When we desire such participation, we take risks. To ask a unit leader to seek feedback from the staff is to risk criticism; for a secretary to tell the department chair about the problems in the unit also creates problems if the climate is not one in which respect for one's opinion is considered essential.

I am highlighting here what was underscored in virtually every case study: individuals desire to have meaningful participation in an institution, but they fear or resist the personal or professional consequences. A gay faculty member will not speak about himself honestly in an environment in which his personal freedom is to be challenged. Faculty will resist working on a strategic plan if they feel it is yet another administrative attempt to foist an idea on the college. Both founding faculty and newer faculty can hide behind the push of bureaucratic paperwork if they have not created arenas where self-reflective dialogue is honored.

Reconsider Promotion and Tenure. I raise this point with hesitation. I am fully aware of the history of promotion and tenure and how policies have been guarantors for academic freedom. Increasingly, however, I feel that as contexts change, so might the manner in which we develop essential protection of faculty inquiry. Are there alternate methods for ensuring academic freedom that loosen the ties of a rigid system that creates a caste of haves and have-nots? Patrick Hill elaborates:

An end to the currently inhibiting system of rank, tenure, and promotion [is necessary]. I am not saying flatly that the whole system must be abandoned, but if it is not, then ways must be found to conduct the conversations of respect fully within the curriculum but entirely without consequences one way or another for promotion-and-tenure decisions (1991, p. 46).

Deep Springs was able to create an effective learning environment without discussions of promotion and tenure; in contrast, the promotion-and-tenure system is a matter of concern at San Marcos; and at Sherman, younger faculty felt they needed to be quiet at faculty meetings so that the tenured faculty could voice their opinions. Gay faculty noted that tenure was the single greatest factor for their silence. Like Hill, I am not certain that we need to do away with promotion and tenure, but I am convinced that serious dialogues need to develop around a system that has created such sharp delineations of power. If we agree, for example, that a democratic community revolves around the participation of all parties, and if we concur that individual and group assessment needs to take place, then surely we need to question a system that many view as arbitrary and capricious. Is it possible for an individual to honestly confront someone who will eventually determine whether the individual gains lifelong employment? I have not sufficiently answered that question, but I raise the issue here with an eye toward the creation of dialogues about it, for I know that the promotion-and-tenure process as it is currently configured works against agape and hope.

Classrooms

Focus on the Nature and Climate of the Classroom. We have too often divorced pedagogy from the curriculum as if there is little or no relationship between the two. Discussions about the "canon" have focused primarily on what is taught. By and large, we have ignored the curricular and pedagogic practices that occur in the natural sciences or in the professions such as engineering and business. We have fought over what should be taught at the expense of how we teach. And yet, we know from the Deep Springs experience how closely pedagogy is tied to the curriculum.

The suggestion here is to confront more forcefully issues that pertain to the nature of the classroom and its climate. By nature, I mean those structural relations that exist in a classroom that frame student-teacher interaction. By climate, I mean the immediate, contextual relations that develop among specific individuals in a class. An analysis of either a classroom's nature or climate without the other is insufficient insofar as classes get defined in terms of their historical and situational circumstances.

A classroom based on the idea of cultural learning and dangerous memory has different demands from the monocultural classroom of the past. In large part, we need to mirror what I have suggested for the organization. We struggle to create an environment where different voices are heard and everyone is a learner. Tolerable discomfort is possible in a classroom as long as the legitimacy of no one is brought into question, and students feel free enough to express their ideas without being punished by low grades or other forms of retribution.

To create a climate of tolerance and respect necessitates reaching out to diverse viewpoints and ensuring that a syllabus reflects that diversity. I am arguing that when the context of the classroom changes, when we teach to students rather than the text, many of the texts will change as well. And if we respect diversity in opinion and background, then we must also have a wide array of authors represented in the syllabus. A conservative critique of such a suggestion, of course, would argue that I am advocating "watering down the curriculum" so that women and people of color are represented as authors; correspondingly, I am demonstrating a concern for students rather than high standards, and ultimately, low standards will hurt those students I want to help. The failure of such arguments is that they fall into the either-or trap—one can have standards or multiculturalism, one can have high expectations or allow minority students into the classroom. Rather than minimalist standards, I am suggesting that the highest possible standards be created in classrooms of difference and hope, but that such classrooms, by definition, take into account those whom they teach and what is taught. Learning is active, collaborative, and concerned with enabling students to come to grips with their own realities and the worlds that they will inhabit.

Generate New Forms of Knowledge. Over the last thirty years, we have seen the explosion of new forms of knowledge so that departments, program areas, and courses in black studies, women's studies, Native American studies and the like have grown increasingly. Except at a handful of institutions, however, these programs are not well established. One fear is that in times of retrenchment, such as now, those areas that are not well endowed will be "downsized," or abolished.

One other argument has been whether concerns such as African American studies or Asian studies should be departments unto themselves or areas of inquiry within a wide number of traditional departments. At San Marcos, we saw the movement toward departmental status. At Sherman, we heard about the establishment of women's studies. The gay faculty pointed out that Normal State had not legitimated any area of inquiry for lesbian and gay studies. Accordingly, the suggestion here is that both areas of inquiry are needed. In keeping with this idea we need traditional academic areas and faculty to increase their involvement and concern for emerging areas of study. In so doing, faculty members might embark on workshops, curricular integration seminars, and in-service lectures about how to change curricula so that faculty become more inclusive with regard to what they teach, how they teach, and who they teach.

At present there are substantial organizational disincentives for faculty to become engaged in seminars and workshops about pedagogy. As I noted in the previous section, promotion and tenure in virtually every type of institution reward research more than teaching. We noted such comments at San Marcos, and we heard little discussion about teaching at Sherman. If we are to create a classroom climate that honors diversity, it is essential that those who teach those classes find the support and incentives to become engaged in understanding the changed nature of their twenty-first-century classrooms.

At the same time, we need codified areas of inquiry such as lesbian and gay studies so that it is possible to concentrate fully and forcefully on emerging areas of knowledge. People need arenas in which they might become articulate in their projects. As noted earlier, when we encourage such areas to grow, we are developing points of resistance in the community that will help the institution to develop viewpoints different from the norm.

Lessen Authority in the Classroom. Given the circumscribed status of a teacher in a classroom, students and faculty will never be equal learners. However, we can make vast strides toward lessening the authority that a teacher exhibits toward students. I began this chapter by quoting Stuart Hall about the need for individuals to position themselves. In a diverse classroom, a first step might be in discussing and accepting the positionality of the participants. In so doing, we give prominence to all individuals and highlight the teacher's own position. I offer this point to highlight how a border intellectual might function in a classroom. That is, we do not create a culture of superiority in which the teacher holds more knowledge than everyone else because we honor other forms of knowing that the teacher will not have, and we also give prominence to organic forms of knowledge.

When we lessen authority, we open the possibility for disagreement and conflict. To enable individuals to speak from their own experiences as well as the text under study suggests that different forms of knowing exist and that we will discover that strong feelings accompany them. Rather than paper over differences or try to suppress them, the border intellectual learns to deal with them. Teaching in this vein is hard because it centers on the constantly changing configurations of the classroom. Rather than arenas such as massive lecture halls where students are silently transmitted information, the classroom becomes an active learning center where everyone participates. The implications for this suggestion reach from English classes to engineering classes, from teachers in history classes to faculty in the hard sciences. For if authority is lessened and positionality is a necessity, then all teaching is fundamentally reconfigured, and teachers are different from the portrait of faculty as experts whose task is to transmit data.

One example of a reconfigured classroom might be where students help develop or change the syllabus at the start of, and during, the term. Students could also be assigned the task of cofacilitator with the instructor, where the student and teacher equally share in the creation of the day's activities.

The development of teamwork and collaboration enables students to work with one another rather than against each other. Obviously, counter-examples can be given, situations in which teacher and student are cofacilitators on paper, but the structure of the class has not changed. My point here, however, is to argue for the development of classroom practices that enable students to have experiences that are more participatory and that enable them to come to terms with their own and others' lives.

And if everyone participates in the development of the course, then we also need to develop formats for evaluation that honor student input. Such a suggestion goes far beyond the simplistic formula of a standard questionnaire generated at the end of the term. Instead, in keeping with the suggestions made about organizational assessment, formative rather than summative evaluations are employed. We create dialogues throughout the course about how we believe the class is proceeding, why we hold these opinions, what can be improved upon, and what must be changed.

Understand the Other. In large part, one of the central points of this text has been to argue for the understanding of other people's realities. I have pointed out how presidents and administrators might embark on activities through which they become cultural learners, and I have offered ideas about how we encourage dangerous memory to develop. Perhaps the most potent arena for learning about one another is in the context of a classroom.

Mark Chesler and Ximena Zuniga (1991), for example, created a classroom project in their sociology course to explore students' attitudes about homophobia. In conducting the exercise, a group of heterosexual students in the class were asked to a wear a pink triangle for a day. In subsequent classroom discussions, heated arguments arose about different individuals' beliefs and attitudes toward sexuality. This class project and discussion offers but one example of an environment in which oppression and discrimination can be at least minimally experienced, and students can feel comfortable enough to speak about their attitudes, fears, and disagreements.

Further, in our understanding of the Other, we must strive not to essentialize an individual as if a gay male or an Asian female speaks for all gay males or all Asian females. Indeed, Asian Americans are often expected to speak for all Asian Americans, as if Asia contained but one culture. To understand the Other necessitates that we come to terms with individuals in their full complement of activities, strengths, and weaknesses. It does not mean that when a discussion of racism occurs, only black students speak, or that when we speak of disabilities, only the physically challenged talk. To do so silences other people in the classroom and essentializes particular groups of students as if they are cultural experts and we turn to them only for one form of knowing. Instead, I am suggesting that we develop creative classroom strategies that enable students to see one another in their full array of diverse identities.

Develop Self-reflection in Faculty. In postsecondary institutions, teaching is often a solitary activity. At Deep Springs, we heard teachers speak about students and the creation of knowledge, but in most of the other cases teaching seemed to be tangential. Faculty may speak to one another about one student, but discussions in general do not revolve around teaching practices. At Sherman, faculty sat in on classes only as an evaluative exercise for untenured faculty. At San Marcos, the lives of faculty were taken up with so much other activity that the idea that they would watch one another's teaching would have been met with disbelief.

To create faculty who are cultural learners, we do not concentrate only on an external understanding of different realities but we also bring into question our own notions of the world, and in particular, our ideas about teaching and learning. To create such an environment, both a culture and incentives need to be created and fostered. Departments might develop coteaching assignments where one teacher is the primary instructor and another individual works out a plan for regular involvement in the classroom. If assessment is formative and nonhierarchical, a series of letters or journals might be created between coteachers so that they are able to talk to one another not only in formalized settings such as meetings but in other ways as well. In turn, primary faculty might describe their teaching to one another and ask for feedback. The role of such action is nicely summarized by John Smyth in a series of questions:

What do my practices say about my assumptions, values, and beliefs about teaching?

Where did these ideas come from?

What social practices are expressed in these ideas?

What causes me to maintain my theories?

What views of power do they embody?

Whose interests seem to be served in my practices?

What constrains my view of what is possible in teaching? (1992, p. 299).

In other words, the development of self-reflection in teaching brings into question the faculty's relationship to what is learned and who is taught. By constantly reevaluating our own position in the teaching and learning process, we force ourselves to learn about ourselves, to create our own dangerous memory, and, in turn, to help develop a community of difference.

CONCLUSION

In *Yearning*, bell hooks has written, "Resistance begins with people confronting pain, whether it's theirs or somebody else's, and wanting to do something to change it" (1990, p. 215). The language hooks uses may be familiar to those of us involved in social movements, but it undoubtedly strikes many individuals as odd when we speak about the problems in the academy in such a manner. Fiscal shortfalls or the creation of new programs generally call on the cold, rational discourse of decision making and management. Even the intellectual debates about what should be taught in our colleges are not defined in terms of understanding one another's sorrows, hopes, and joys.

I have argued in this text, however, that understanding one another's pain and one another's views of the world and community are essential for academic institutions as we approach the next century. Education concerns the ability of people to come to terms with their own and others' identities, and to understand how the world shapes and is shaped by social interaction. And such knowledge is not merely to be learned for learning's sake; rather, it is to be employed in the work of building democracy—in our organizations, in our communities, and in our nation.

The challenge for college and university participants is to develop concepts of the organization and the classroom that enable us to enact this form of education. The models we carry with us in large part shape how we act. If we subscribe to abstract notions of truth, we act one way, and if we accept the idea of agape, we act another way. One model defines students, administrators, and teachers in one form, and the other model employs a radically different interpretation.

Critical postmodernism leaves us perhaps with as many questions as answers, and it should. Border intellectuals ought not rely on road maps to the future, for the territory is unmarked and alien. We are unable any longer to venture forward as a postmodern Christopher Columbus intent on discovering a "new world" and content with the knowledge that a home awaits us upon our return. Rather, we continue in our academic communities as democratic citizens involved in creating the hope that we have yet to realize. The fixed territories of home no longer exist, and yet we have one another with whom to build our academic communities of the next century.

References

Abbey, E. (1971). *Desert solitaire, a season in the wilderness.* New York: Ballantine Books.

Anzaldua, G. (1987). *Borderlands, La frontera.* San Francisco: Spinsters/Aunt Lute.

Benhabib, S. (1986). *Critique, norm, and utopia.* New York: Columbia University Press.

Bensimon, E. M. (1991, November). *Lesbian existence and the challenge to normative constructions of the academy.* Paper presented at the meeting of the Association for the Study of Higher Education, Boston, MA.

Bensimon, E. M. (1992). Personal correspondence.

Bensimon, E. M., & Neumann, A. (1993). *Redesigning collegiate leadership: Teams and teamwork in higher education.* Baltimore: Johns Hopkins University Press.

Berube, A. (1990). *Coming out under fire: The history of gay men and women in World War II.* New York: Free Press.

Birnbaum, R. (1988). *How colleges work.* San Francisco: Jossey-Bass.

Bloom, A. (1987). *The closing of the American mind.* New York: Simon and Schuster.

Bowen, H. R., & Schuster, J. H. (1986). *American professors: A national resource imperiled.* New York: Oxford University Press.

Boyer, E. L. (1990). *Campus life: In search of community.* Princeton, NJ: The Carnegie Foundation for the Advancement of Teaching.

Burbules, N. C., & Rice, S. (1991). Dialogue across differences: Continuing the conversation. *Harvard Educational Review, 61*(4), 393–416.

Chaffee, E. E. (1984). Successful strategic management in small private colleges. *Journal of Higher Education, 55,* 212–241.

_____. (1985). Three models of strategy. *Academy of Management Review, 10,* 89–98.

_____. (1989). Strategy and effectiveness in systems of higher education. In J. Smart (Ed.), *Higher education: Handbook of theory and research* (Vol. 5) (pp. 1–30). New York: Agathon Press.

Chesler, M. A., & Zuniga, X. (1991). Dealing with prejudice and conflict in the classroom: The pink triangle exercise. *Teaching Sociology, 19,* 173–181.

Clark, B. R. (1970). *The distinctive college.* Chicago: Aldine.

_____. (1980). The making of an organizational saga. In H. J. Leavitt & L. R. Pondy (Eds.), *Readings in managerial psychology* (2d ed.) (pp. 233–262). Chicago: University of Chicago Press.

_____. (1987). *The academic life.* Princeton, NJ: The Carnegie Foundation for the Advancement of Teaching.

Cohen, M. D., & March, J. G. (1974). *Leadership and ambiguity: The American college president.* New York: McGraw-Hill.

Collins, P. H. (1986). Learning from the outsider within: The sociological significance of black feminist thought. *Social Problems, 33*(6), 14–32.

_____. (1991). *Black feminist thought: Knowledge, consciousness and the politics of empowerment.* New York: Routledge.

D'Augelli, A. (1989). Lesbians' and gay men's experiences of discrimination and harassment in a university community. *American Journal of Community Psychology, 17,* 317–321.

Dewey, J. (1966). *Democracy and education.* New York: The Free Press.

D'Souza, D. (1991). *Illiberal education: The politics of race and sex on campus.* New York: The Free Press.

Duberman, M. (1972). *Black Mountain: An exploration in community.* New York: E. P. Dutton.

Ellsworth, E. (1989). Why doesn't this feel empowering? Working through the repressive myths of critical pedagogy. *Harvard Educational Review, 59*(3), 297–324.

Ewell, P. T. (1991). Assessment and TQM: In search of convergence. In L. A. Sherr & D. J. Teeter (Eds.), *Total quality management in higher education* (pp. 39–52). New Directions for Institutional Research, No. 71. San Francisco: Jossey-Bass.

Fay, B. (1987). *Critical social science.* Ithaca, NY: Cornell University Press.

Foster, W. (1986). *Paradigms and promises: New approaches to educational administration.* Buffalo, NY: Prometheus Books.

Foucault, M. (1973). The intellectuals and power: A discussion between Michel Foucault and Gilles Deleuze. *Telos, 16,* 103–109.

_____. (1980a). *Power/knowledge: Selected interviews and other writings 1972–1977.* New York: Pantheon Books.

_____. (1980b). *The history of sexuality, volume I: An introduction* (R. Hurley, Trans.). New York: Vintage Books.

Friend, R. A. (1992). Choices, not closets: Heterosexism and homophobia in schools. In L. Weis & M. Fine (Eds.), *Silenced voices: Issues of class, race and gender in today's schools* (pp. 209-236). Albany, NY: State University of New York Press.

Geertz, C. (1983). Blurred genres: The refiguration of social thought. In C. Geertz, *Local knowledge* (pp. 19–35). New York: Basic Books.

Gergen, K. J. (1991). *The saturated self: Dilemmas of identity in contemporary life.* New York: Basic Books.

Giroux, H. A. (1983). *Theory and resistance in education: A pedagogy for the opposition.* South Hadley, MA: Bergin & Garvey.

_____. (1988a). *Schooling and the struggle for public life.* Minneapolis, MN: University of Minnesota Press.

_____. (1988b). Border pedagogy in the age of postmodernism. *Journal of Education, 170*(3), 162–181.

_____. (1990). The politics of postmodernism. *Journal of Urban and Cultural Studies, 1*(1), 5–38.

_____. (1992). *Border crossings: Cultural workers and the politics of education.* New York: Routledge.

_____. (forthcoming). Paulo Freire and the politics of postcolonialism. In P. McLaren & P. Leonard (Eds.), *Paulo Freire: A critical encounter.* New York: Routledge.

Gitlin, T. (1989). Postmodernism defined, at last. *Utne Reader, 34*, 52–61.

Glenn, T. (1991). *Factions, community, and the individual: An ethnography of Deep Springs.* Unpublished manuscript.

Goffman, E. (1967). *Interaction ritual.* New York: Pantheon Books.

Gorman, T. (1992, May 10). CSUSM told to push for innovation. *Los Angeles Times*, pp. B1, B3.

Gramsci, A. (1971). *Selections from the prison notebooks.* London: Lawrence & Wishart.

Hall, S. (1990). Cultural identity and diaspora. In J. Rutherford (Ed.), *Identity: Community, culture, difference* (pp. 222–237). London: Lawrence & Wishart.

Hartsock, N. (1979). Feminist theory and revolutionary strategy. In Z. Eisenstein (Ed.), *Capitalist patriarchy and the case for socialist feminism.* New York: Monthly Review Press.

Heath, S. B. (1983). *Ways with words, language, life, and work in communities and classrooms.* New York: Cambridge University Press.

Herek, G. (1989). Hate crimes against lesbians and gay men: Issues for research and social policy. *American Psychologist, 44*, 933–940.

Hill, P. J. (1991). Multiculturalism: The crucial philosophical and organizational issues. *Change, 23*(4), 38–47.

Hill, S. (1991). Ethnicity: Identity and difference. *Radical America, 13*(4), 9–20.

hooks, b. (1989). *Talking back.* Boston: South End Press.

_____. (1990). *Yearning.* Boston: South End Press.

Jaggar, A. M. (1989). Love and knowledge: Emotion in feminist epistemology. In A. M. Jaggar & S. R. Bordo (Eds.), *Gender/body/knowledge: Feminist reconstructions of being and knowing* (pp. 145–171). New Brunswick: Rutgers University Press.

Katz, J. (1976). *Gay American history.* New York: Crowell.

Katz, M. (1987). *Reconstructing American education.* Cambridge, MA: Harvard University Press.

Keller, G. (1983). *Academic strategy.* Baltimore: Johns Hopkins University Press.

Kimball, R. (1990). *Tenured radicals: How politics has corrupted our higher education.* New York: Harper & Row.

King, M. L., Jr. (1958). *Stride toward freedom.* New York: Harper & Row.

LaSalle, L. A., & Rhoads, R. A. (1992, April). *Exploring campus intolerance: A textual analysis of comments concerning gay, lesbian, and bisexual persons.* Paper presented at the annual conference for the American Association of Educational Researchers, San Francisco, CA.

Lather, P. (1989). Postmodernism and the politics of enlightenment. *Educational Foundations, 3*(3), 8–9.

Light, R. J. (1992). *The Harvard assessment seminars: Explorations with students and faculty about teaching, learning, and student life* (2d report). Cambridge, MA: Harvard University Graduate School of Education and Kennedy School of Government.

Lorde, A. (1984). *Sister outsider.* Freedom, CA: The Crossing Press.

_____. (1985). *I am your sister: Black women organizing across sexualities.* Latham, NY: Kitchen Table Press.

Marchese, T. (1991). TQM reaches the academy. *AAHE Bulletin, 44*(3), 3–9.

McLaren, P. (forthcoming). Multiculturalism and the postmodern critique: Towards a pedagogy of resistance and transformation. *Cultural Studies.*

Merton, R. (1968). *Social theory and social structure.* New York: Wiley.

Mohanty, C. T. (1989–1990). On race and voice: Challenges for liberal education in the 1990s. *Cultural Critique, 14,* 179–208.

Olson, C. (1966). The kingfishers. In R. Creeley (Ed.), *Selected writings of Charles Olson* (pp. 167–173). New York: New Directions.

Outka, G. (1972). *Agape: An ethical analysis.* New Haven, CT: Yale University Press.

Plant, R. (1986). *The pink triangle: The Nazi war against homosexuals.* New York: Henry Holt.

Ravitch, D. (1990). Multiculturalism. *The American Scholar, 59*(3) 337–354.

Rich, A. (1986). *Blood, bread, and poetry: Selected prose 1979–1985.* New York: W. W. Norton.

Rosaldo, R. (1989). *Culture and truth.* Boston: Beacon Press.

Rutherford, J. (1990). A place called home: Identity and the cultural politics of difference. In J. Rutherford (Ed.), *Identity: Community, culture, difference* (pp. 9–27). London: Lawrence & Wishart.

Sedgwick, E. K. (1990). *Epistemology of the closet.* Berkeley: University of California Press.

Smyth, J. (1992). Teachers' work and the politics of reflection. *American Educational Research Journal, 29*(2), 267–300.

Tannen, D. (1990). *You just don't understand, men and women in conversation.* New York: Morrow.

Tierney, W. G. (1988a). *The web of leadership.* Greenwich, CT: JAI Press.

———. (1988b). Organizational culture in higher education. *Journal of Higher Education, 59*(1), 2–21.

———. (1989). *Curricular landscapes, democratic vistas: Transformative leadership in higher education.* New York: Praeger.

———. (1991). Ideology and identity in postsecondary institutions. In W. G. Tierney (Ed.), *Culture and ideology in higher education* (pp. 35–57). New York: Praeger.

———. (1992a). Building academic communities of difference. *Change, 24*(2), 41–46.

———. (1992b). *Official encouragement, institutional discouragement: Minorities in academe—the Native American experience.* Norwood, NJ: Ablex.

———. (forthcoming a). On method and hope. In A. Gitlin (Ed.), *Power and method.* New York: Routledge.

———. (forthcoming b). Self and identity in a postmodern world: A life story. In D. McLaughlin & W. G. Tierney (Eds.), *Naming silenced lives.* New York: Routledge.

Tierney, W. G., & Rhoads, R. A. (forthcoming a). Postmodernism and critical theory in higher education: Implications for research and practice. In J. C. Smart (Ed.), *Higher education: Handbook of theory and research.* New York: Agathon.

———. (forthcoming b). The culture of assessment. In J. Smyth (Ed.), *The changing labour process in higher education.* London: Open University Press.

Tompkins, J. (1987). Me and my shadow. *New Literary History, 19*(1), 169–178.

———. (1990). Pedagogy of the distressed. *College English, 52*(6), 653–660.

Weeks, J. (1990). The value of difference. In J. Rutherford (Ed.), *Identity: Community, culture, difference* (pp. 88–100). London: Lawrence & Wishart.

Welch, S. D. (1990). *A feminist ethic of risk.* Minneapolis, MN: Fortress Press.

Williams, W. L. (1992). *The spirit and the flesh: Sexual diversity in American Indian culture.* Boston: Beacon Press.

Index

About the Author

WILLIAM G. TIERNEY is Associate Professor in the College of Education, and Senior Research Associate in the Center for the Study of Higher Education at Pennsylvania State University. He is the author of four books, including *Curricular Landscapes, Democratic Vistas* (Praeger, 1989) and the editor of many more.